SpringerBriefs in Social Work

SpringerBriefs present concise summaries of cutting-edge research and practical applications. Featuring compact volumes of 55 to 125 pages, the series covers a range of content from professional to academic. Typical topics might include:

- A timely report of state-of-the art analytical techniques
- A bridge between new research results, as published in journal articles, and a contextual literature review
- A snapshot of a hot or emerging topic
- An in-depth case study or clinical example
- A presentation of core concepts that students must understand in order to make independent contributions

SpringerBriefs in Social Work showcases emerging theory, empirical research, and practical applications in a wide variety of topics in social work and related areas. Briefs are characterized by fast, global electronic dissemination and expedited production schedules.

Louise Whitaker • Katherine Reid • Emma Tseris • Hollie Ballingall • Ashlea Borg • Binti Jones • Alex Olsen • Aimee Pitt • Lisa Thorpy

Social Work in the Mental Health Field

From Power Analysis to Practice

Springer

Louise Whitaker
Social Work, Faculty of Health
Southern Cross University
Coolangatta, QLD, Australia

Emma Tseris
Social Work and Policy Studies
Faculty of Arts and Social Sciences
The University of Sydney
Sydney, NSW, Australia

Ashlea Borg
Social Worker
Dharug Land, NSW, Australia

Alex Olsen
Social Worker
Turrbal and Yuggera Country
QLD, Australia

Lisa Thorpy
Social Worker
Yaegl and Bundjalung Lands
NSW, Australia

Katherine Reid
Faculty of Health
School of Public Health and Social Work
Queensland University of Technology
Kelvin Grove, QLD, Australia

Hollie Ballingall
Mental Health Social Worker
Gadigal Land, NSW, Australia

Binti Jones
Social Worker
Bundjalung Country
NSW, Australia

Aimee Pitt
Social Worker
Bundjalung Country
NSW, Australia

ISSN 2195-3104 ISSN 2195-3112 (electronic)
SpringerBriefs in Social Work

ISBN 978-3-032-08305-0 ISBN 978-3-032-08306-7 (eBook)
https://doi.org/10.1007/978-3-032-08306-7

This Springer imprint is published by the registered company Springer Nature Switzerland AG
The registered company address is: Gewerbestrasse 11, 6330 Cham, Switzerland

Competing Interests The authors do not have any competing financial or non-financial interests to declare.

Ethics Approval The research was approved by Griffith University Human Research Ethics Committee.

About the Book

This book provides a contemporary and practical resource for exploring critical social work practices in mental health. It explores how a power analysis can be enacted, through a variety of skills and actions, in order to navigate complex organisational and social contexts and make a difference in the mental health field.

Mental health social work is contested and complex. While it is widely accepted that social workers should bring a social justice lens to their practice, it is often unclear how an analysis of power influences and is applied in the minutiae of everyday practice. Social workers might settle into complacency, making rhetorical commitments to 'person-centred' and 'trauma-informed' approaches that are not meaningfully connected to actions, or they might find themselves complying with dominant colonial and biomedical agendas in an attempt to gain professional legitimacy within healthcare teams.

Beyond naming the tensions and competing values faced by social workers in mental health contexts, this book explores concrete examples of working towards justice in solidarity with people and communities experiencing distress. Through a collaboration between three social work researchers and six social workers currently working in the field, this book offers a unique perspective. Areas covered include: the complexities of working in biomedical and neoliberal environments; addressing White privilege; noticing and responding to epistemic injustices; multidisciplinary teamwork; systemic advocacy; the politics of language; elevating socio-political contexts and lived experience knowledges and navigating risk paradigms.

Social Work in the Mental Health Field: From Power Analysis to Practice is relevant to social work students and educators, as it moves beyond micro–macro binary thinking, through exploring how social workers have aimed to enact practices that are informed by a power analysis in mental health settings. Examples are provided across the contexts of individual direct practice, group work, community work, systems change, and private practice. This book is pertinent to new and experienced social workers who are seeking an accessible and contemporary resource to reflect on their practice and to explore ways of working towards social justice in the mental health field.

Contents

About the Authors

Louise Whitaker, PhD, MSW, BSW is an Associate Professor in Social Work at Southern Cross University, Australia.

Katherine Reid, PhD, BSW, BA, GradDipNT is a Senior Lecturer in social work at the Queensland University of Technology, Australia.

Emma Tseris, PhD, BSW, BA is an Associate Professor in social work and policy studies at the University of Sydney, Australia.

Hollie Ballingall is a Yuin woman, raised on Dharawal Country, now living and working on Gadigal Land. She is an Accredited Mental Health Social Worker who holds a Bachelor of Arts (Psychology), a Master of Social Work (Qualifying), and a Graduate Certificate in Youth Mental Health.

Ashlea Borg, BSW is a critical social worker with experience working in community and government contexts.

Binti Jones, MSW, BA is a casual academic with Southern Cross University, Australia, and a social worker with several years of experience in community services work across social housing, homelessness, mental health, and family services.

Alex Olsen, BA, BSW has held a variety of social work positions within non-government and government organisations both in Australia and the UK.

Aimee Pitt, BSW, BA is a social worker whose work has supported individuals, groups, and communities navigating distress and marginalisation.

Lisa Thorpy, MSW, BA is a casual academic with Southern Cross University, Australia, who has worked in a variety of social work and policy positions in mental health and violence abuse and neglect.

Chapter 1
Examining Mental Health Social Work: From Power Analysis to Practice

Introduction

Social work in the mental health field is challenging, complex, and contested. While the social justice brief of the profession is clear, its enactment is not straightforward. Social and institutional contexts dominated by ways of thinking privileging those in positions of power, including colonialism, patriarchy, managerialism, and biomedicine make the enactment challenging. This book investigates how social work can not only **conceptualise and critically analyse** patterns of power in mental health, but how such analysis can be **applied** in practice in the field. We acknowledge the nuanced skills and practices involved in destabilising taken-for-granted power arrangements, doing subversive work, navigating competing paradigms, and fostering socially just mental health systems. Beyond merely describing the contradictions and complexities, this book offers rich practice examples that demonstrate how social workers seek to make a difference, and resist, even in small ways, the dominance of biomedical neoliberalism in the mental health field. Examples include unsettling 'illness' paradigms, identifying the links between social injustices and distress, challenging risk aversion, advocacy, disrupting colonial legacies, engaging with First Nations knowledges, and moving beyond individual-focused work towards community work. The inquiry that inspired this book set out to investigate contemporary social work practice focused on embodying, enacting, and promoting 'social change and development, social cohesion, and the empowerment and liberation of people… (following) principles of social justice, human rights, collective responsibility and respect for diversities' (IFSW, 2014) in the mental health field.

The social work practice discussed in this book was unveiled through a practice research partnership where a group of mental health social workers collaborated as co-researchers and co-subjects individually and collectively critically reflecting on experiences of their practice in this field. Nine women who are currently engaged in

L. Whitaker et al., *Social Work in the Mental Health Field*, SpringerBriefs in Social Work, https://doi.org/10.1007/978-3-032-08306-7_1

social work in the field of mental health in Australia came together through a shared interest in how social work's espoused values of social justice can be meaningfully enacted within contemporary mental health settings, towards exploring the nuances and complexities of what it means to bridge critical theory and practice in mental health social work.

Throughout the book, we refer to an analysis of power. There are many ways that power and power relationships can be understood. Critical theories point to enduring systems and social structures that create and reinforce unequal power relationships. Power, in this sense, is oppressive. While we recognise that people are both supported by, and can be victims of, systems and institutional processes that exert power over them, we also understand 'where there is power, there is resistance … a multiplicity of points of resistance' (Foucault, 1978, p.95). In this way, power can be productive. It is important to note that we are not separate from power as social workers, because it is present in every interaction we have. In this sense, 'power means relations, a more-or-less organised, hierarchical coordinated cluster of relations' (Foucault, 1980, p.198). This understanding is important in contextualising the matrix of power relations within the mental health system. Such power relations 'rely on calculated and rational programs or forms of knowledge' (Lemke, 2016, p.18). In this book, we acknowledge that social work is embedded in these socio-political systems and investigate social work practice accounting for, and moving beyond, dominant knowledge systems and practices in the field of mental health.

Research, including social work scholarship, has highlighted the need for a significant re-orientation towards social justice in mental health, in response to an increasing emphasis on individual-focused, symptom-management approaches within Western mental health systems (Whitaker et al., 2021; United Nations Human Rights Office of the High Commissioner, 2017). Achieving this shift is not straightforward, given the highly managerial and medicalised organisational contexts of mental health services (Dawson et al., 2020). Within such settings, socio-political factors are largely invisibilised—concealed underneath the language of 'length of stay' and 'diagnosis'—leading to a focus on 'treating disorders' within individuals (Dawson et al., 2020; Hendrix et al., 2021). In this chapter, we highlight the profound influences of dominant socio-political systems of capitalism, Whiteness, managerialism, and biomedicine on the ways in which mental distress is conceptualised, before describing the complex position of social work as an agent of these systems while instigating their change. This chapter concludes by describing the research that inspired this book.

Neoliberalism and Capitalism: Is the Person the Problem?

Concerns about the profound influences of global conflict and environmental disasters, poverty, the ongoing impacts of the COVID-19 pandemic, the rising costs of living, and social isolation on experiences of distress are well-documented (World Health Organisation, 2025). Referring to the underlying and harmful influence of global capitalism, Capra and Luisi (2016) map intersecting environmental factors influencing everyday lives. These include a self-amplifying feedback loop of population growth and poverty; threats to food security associated with excessive consumption and waste; and economic inequality and a breakdown of democracy. At the heart of this is the 'illusion that unlimited growth is possible on a finite planet' where our 'current economic system ... [is]... fuelled by materialism and greed' (Capra & Luisi, 2016, p.365). In a contemporary context, the emotional impacts of these factors are usually referred to using the term 'mental health', but the language of mental health can invisibilise the broader socio-political contexts, and the underpinning power relations of patriarchy, neoliberalism, colonialism, and racism, which intersect with and are fuelled by global capitalism leading to environmental destruction. As authors, we concur that the worth of human beings is not indicated by how much we produce, and that we need to challenge 'grind culture' arising from a 'collaboration between white supremacy and capitalism' (Hersey, 2022, p.14). The features of global capitalism foster distress, but the very systems that have been developed to address distress—diagnosis; individual treatment; notions of mental health that overlap with 'rational' and 'productive' citizenship—also sit within the frame of capitalism, where the insidiousness of economic rationalism conceals the influences of oppressive social structures (Cohen, 2016; Moncrieff, 2022).

Stemming from the philosophical assumptions of capitalism, neoliberalism focuses on the reduction of the welfare state, with the aim to centre the 'free' market (Stark, 2018). Neoliberalism has increased in dominance, positioning the ideal individual as a responsible productive citizen who self-manages their own 'mental health', irrespective of the social injustices they may experience (Brown, 2021; Reid & Alford, 2023). The neoliberal regime has given rise to and supports biomedical approaches as the most legitimate means to respond to social concerns. By focusing on the individual and potential 'internal pathology', matters of social inequality and injustice are 'biomedicalized and depoliticized [with an] emphasis on disorders, diagnosis, and mental illness' (Brown, 2021, p.646). Biomedical approaches, which situate distress as a medical condition, decontextualise and overlook the oppressive forces the individual may be facing, leaving structural factors unaddressed and maintaining the status quo (Brown, 2021; Moncrieff, 2022; Reid, 2023). The individual is expected to self-regulate and be 'resilient' regardless of the socio-cultural and political context, and with little attention given to the ways in which notions of resilience and self-regulation are informed by White, Western understandings of ideal personhood—they are not neutral or universal concepts of wellbeing.

Decentring Whiteness in Mental Health

While steps have been taken to acknowledge the harms of oppressive paradigms in mental health, including patriarchy, neoliberalism, and biomedicalism, there are ongoing, troubling silences in considering Whiteness in the mental health field. The mental health field is permeated by settler-colonial knowledges and the subjugation of Indigenous Knowledge Systems (Dudgeon, 2020). For example, the discourse of 'cultural competence' is focused on the development of skills to work with 'the Other' (Tascon & Gatwiri, 2020). This paradigm conceals Whiteness, justifying the ongoing dominance of White, Western understandings of 'mental health', and maintaining the power of mental health professionals (van Noppen et al., 2024). It has been noted that mental health systems pathologise First Nations people, as a tactic of colonial power, with a persistent focus on deficits within individuals (Moreton-Robinson, 2015; Wright et al., 2024). Diagnostic paradigms are predicated on a mind/body dualism and a preoccupation with 'rational' selfhood, discounting the role of community, culture, and Country in sustaining collective wellbeing (Milroy et al., 2024). These paradigms, therefore, produce significant harm for First Nations people and communities.

When biomedical interpretations of distress and resistance locate 'problems' within individuals, little or no attention is given to addressing systemic conditions and inequities (Mills, 2018). Thus, the continued focus on clinical, diagnostic, standardised, and individual-focused work as the 'gold standard' approach to working with distress conceals the interpersonal, structural, and intergenerational colonial violence in the lives of First Nations people. Consequently, contact with mental health services is frequently re-traumatising for Aboriginal and Torres Strait Islander people (Dudgeon et al., 2017) with social work being drawn into complicity in replicating harm and the silencing of First Nations worldviews.

To add to this, mental health services have been critiqued for becoming preoccupied with tokenistic engagements and 'surface accommodations' (Muller, 2020), for example, using words such as 'yarning' and 'decolonising' in ways that are disconnected from meaningful transformations in the power relations between mental health workers and those on the receiving end of services. It has been noted that the mere 'inclusion' of Indigenous perspectives in mental health organisations, when they continue to be governed by settler-colonial paradigms, does not go nearly far enough; such tokenism can hinder self-determination and prevent First Nations knowledges from being meaningfully embedded into systems design (Wright et al., 2024). Such approaches come from a position of seeing decolonisation as a finite set of actions, rather than as an ongoing process, in response to the insidious and constant process of colonisation (Ryan & Ivelja, 2023). Consequently, actions need to extend beyond the comfort of engaging merely at a rhetorical or superficial level, instead being willing to disrupt Whiteness, to sit with discomfort, to interrogate social work's complicity in racism, and to recognise Aboriginal and Torres Strait Islander sovereignty (Ryan & Ivelja, 2023).

The Dominance of Managerial and Biomedical Discourses in Mental Health

Despite significant increases in resourcing biomedical mental health systems, the lack of evidence regarding improved mental health globally has resulted in calls for an overhaul of current approaches (Davies, 2021). Recognition of the over-medicalisation of mental health is gathering momentum, alongside the acknowledgement of colonising practices within mental health systems, the political nature of mental health care, and the increasing unjustifiability of continued investment in biologically focused mental health research (Frances, 2013; United Nations General Assembly Human Rights Council, 2017; United Nations Human Rights Office of the High Commissioner, 2017). Mental health services struggle to meet demand and even more concerningly, are often not addressing the needs of people experiencing distress, due to a medication-focused perspective (Davies, 2021). The United Nations Special Rapporteur has called for 'little short of a revolution in mental health care to end decades of neglect, abuse and violence… to move away from traditional practices and thinking and enable a long overdue shift to a rights-based approach' (United Nations Human Rights Office of the High Commissioner, 2017). The negative response to such calls for action demonstrate the deeply politicised nature of the field and the ongoing dominance of a biomedical paradigm (Oute & McPherson, 2023). Despite this politicisation, conversations about social work practice in this field often neglect to meaningfully engage with the politics of mental health.

The dominance of biomedical understandings of distress and managerialist approaches to managing services blinkers other views, particularly the perspectives of people interfacing with mental health organisations. Hierarchies of knowledge within multidisciplinary teams frequently subsume socio-political understandings of distress and encourage people living with mental distress and social workers to lean into pervasive perspectives. This insidious dominance of colonial, patriarchal, neoliberal, and biomedical models ultimately led to 'epistemic injustice', whereby people with psychiatric diagnoses are de-legitimated as credible knowers (Daya, 2022; Fricker, 2007). Indigo Daya, a psychiatric survivor, researcher, activist, and artist describes the immense power differentials in mental health systems, which leads to:

> the exclusion of my own ideas about the meaning of this experience, along with the absence of any kind of psychological or social interpretation, of which there could have been many… often resulting in violent practices used against people like myself who express our distress in ways that fall outside of accepted norms, and which attract ableist assumptions about our capacity as knowers or testifiers (Daya, 2022, p.6).

Despite their dominance, diagnostic and biomedical practices cannot be viewed as neutral or unproblematic. Psychiatric diagnoses frequently have devastating, cascading, and ongoing implications across the life course, particularly for people who are navigating multiple coercive systems, such as the legal system and prisons, and child protection systems. The underlying assumption is *the problem is in the person.*

This leads to highly de-contextualised understandings, centring medical treatments and prescriptive therapeutic interventions, while limiting other possible forms of support and resources.

At the same time, it is notable that even more 'progressive' understandings of distress, such as 'trauma-informed care', have also been critiqued as complicit in supporting a medicalised and symptom-oriented approach, which largely disregards the socio-political contexts of people's lives (Helbich & Jabr, 2022). Consequently, while the rhetoric of mental health care has shifted towards more inclusive language and 'strengths-based', 'recovery-oriented' approaches, such reforms seem to have failed to fully grapple with the innate contradiction between the aspirations of 'trauma-informed' paradigms and the ongoing reliance in mental health systems on diagnostic assessments, pharmacological treatments, and individualised therapeutic modalities (Becker-Blease, 2017). As authors, we recognise the importance of transforming the language of mental health, including questioning the usefulness of the term 'mental health' global; focusing on an assessment of individuals, while rendering invisible the contexts of people's lives, including poverty, racism, patriarchy, and institutional violence. However, we also question the over-reliance on language reform, as an insufficient strategy to address significant harms and violence occurring within the contemporary mental health system. We recognise ongoing inquiries over several decades, attempts at implementing reform in mental health systems, have created a rhetoric of 'progress' while obscuring the lack of change in mental health service provision (Francis et al., 2022). In fact, in Australia, there have been over 55 inquires at a national or state level, with key recommendations made 30 years ago to improve the mental health sector still not acted upon (Francis et al., 2022). The research that inspired this book therefore aimed to move beyond superficial engagement with concepts such as 'recovery-oriented, trauma-informed care', to interrogate power arrangements more deeply. For example, as sanitised and linear narratives of 'mental health recovery' often do not reflect the experiences of people interacting with the mental health system (Sinclair & Mahboub, 2024), it is crucial to engage with diverse perspectives and be willing to 'engage and learn from the process of being uncomfortable' (Newcomb & Venning, 2024, p.571). Through challenging certainties and taken-for-granted knowledge hierarchies in the mental health field, it may become possible to begin to 'think otherwise' (Fullagar, 2018) about the current status quo of coercive, biomedical, and rigid therapeutic paradigms, in order to develop a 'resistant imagination—an imagination that is ready to confront relational possibilities that have been lost, ignored, or that remain to be discovered or invented' (Medina, 2013, p.299).

Contesting Understandings of 'Risk'

'Risk' is a pervasive concept within mental health service provision, wherein assessing and responding to 'risk' has become an ingrained and taken-for-granted aspect of contemporary mental health services (Ross, 2020; Whitaker et al., 2021). A strong focus on 'risk' and a surveillance culture in mental health is used to justify intrusive, custodial, unwanted, and harmful interventions (Slemon et al., 2017). Noting the ways in which paternalism, which is pervasive in practice in the mental health field, can be used to conceal and justify social control (Manchester, 2015) and a large body of research exploring service users' perspectives on the extensive harms of coercive practices (Ross, 2020), we take a critical position to analyse how 'risk' is constructed within mainstream mental health services. For example, we interrogate and question the commonplace ideas that:

- risk is located within individuals;
- heightened emotional expression is a form of risk that needs to be managed by mental health workers;
- concerns about risk justify a coercive response by mental health services and;
- attention to risk is a neutral and benevolent component of mental health service provision.

Risk aversion is underpinned by sanist assumptions, which incorrectly position people experiencing distress as 'dangerous' (Daley et al., 2019). Despite a strong narrative about the benevolence of psychiatric services, a preoccupation with 'risk' is so frequently reflective of the interests, priorities, and agendas of mental health organisations (Slemon et al., 2017). This leads to harmful practices, as understanding people as 'risky' is othering and discriminatory (Jacob et al., 2021). Risk discourses create distance between workers and people on the receiving end of services, justifying and normalising the use of force and other oppressive responses, with disproportionate effects on minority groups, including First Nations people (Ross, 2020).

The assessment of 'risk' within individuals reflects the intersections between neoliberalism and Western mental health systems, whereby systemic harms are rendered invisible. Consequently, risk discourses pathologise individuals, while concealing the myriad forms of violence in people's lives, including institutional violence within the mental health system, in addition to the 'slow violence' in people's lives, including poverty and racism (Daley et al., 2019). It has also been noted that a stubborn refusal to engage critically with risk discourses has constrained efforts to meaningfully change the mental health system, drastically reducing the possibilities for transformative shifts in mental health services (Maylea, 2017). Thus, it is important to find ways to articulate a critical perspective on risk and to challenge taken-for-granted assumptions about risk. In our research, we aimed to consider the possibilities that exist for social workers to move beyond pathologising and individualising understandings of 'risk', to hold onto complexity and context, to question risk-averse organisational contexts, and to find spaces and possibilities to respond in ways that uphold people's dignity and rights.

Social Work's Complicity in Harmful System Responses

There are many layers of power that can be identified within Western mental health systems. Many social workers can **identify** social inequities affecting people engaging with the mental health system, and can **recognise** power imbalances regarding a range of issues (Morley & Macfarlane, 2010)—including the power that professionals have over service users; an array of gendered, economic, and racialised oppressions affecting people who have received psychiatric diagnoses; and the pervasive use of coercion within mental health services, in both overt and more subtle forms. However, critical perspectives on mental health can be dismissed as lofty and unrealistic ideals, leading to a disconnect between the espoused rhetoric of social justice and a reliance on medicalised approaches in practice. Therefore, even the most astute power analysis does not automatically lead to transformative practices. It is crucial, then, that social work practice moves on from a mere intellectual engagement with social justice.

In the mental health sector today, social workers are increasingly aligning themselves with clinical approaches to support people experiencing distress, with a focus on diagnostic criteria and rigid therapeutic guidelines and, in ways that fail to reflect a socio-political analysis (Brown, 2021). There may be many reasons for this, including pressure to work in ways that are 'measurable' and able to adhere to Key Performance Indicators (KPIs), or a desire to gain legitimacy or status when working in hierarchical multidisciplinary teams. It may also reflect a narrowing of social work practice in neoliberal times, away from politicised and community-oriented paradigms, towards a focus on becoming a 'mental health clinician', with an emphasis on 'working with individuals' and a technocratic approach (Morley & Macfarlane, 2010). Such practices attempt to make people fit into predetermined categories, using a narrow array of therapeutic 'techniques', which have gained significant traction, due to the claim that they are 'evidence-based'. Such practices are often distanced from an analysis of power and draw on very narrow forms of evidence, while ignoring social theory and lived experience knowledges (Pease, 2020). A preoccupation with measuring 'outcomes' can encourage us to lean into certainty, and to centre social workers as 'experts' in 'fixing individuals', disregarding circumstances perpetuating distress. This encourages an approach that is about enacting 'power over' relationships with people on the receiving end of services, in ways that are detached from social justice values. Consequently, there may be a gap between our espoused theory and our theory-in-use (Savaya & Gardner, 2012).

Diverse Critical Approaches to Social Work Practice in the Mental Health Field

Critical social work is well-established, however, there is no one critical approach to mental health social work. Social workers taking a critical approach bring an understanding of social contexts, the injustices of stigma and discrimination, and the socio-political drivers of distress (Bark et al., 2023; Stone et al., 2021). For Brown (2020), a critical clinical approach focuses on integrating postmodern and critical frameworks including feminist, narrative, anti-racist, postcolonial, and post-modern deconstructive critiques of key concepts such as power, knowledge, experience, self, emotion, and ethics. In Northern Ireland, social workers seek to improve and safeguard social wellbeing, encompassing a quality of relationships and sense of belonging; choice and control; and having purpose and meaning in life, as well as feeling safe and secure (Department of Health, 2019). In Australia, 'social work has a unique and vital role in challenging simplistic, depoliticised individualising constructions of mental health and illness, and in advancing contextualised and holistic understandings of people's experiences' (Morley & Macfarlane, 2010, p. 46). Poole et al. (2012) describe the pressing need for anti-sanist social work practice, providing a compelling call to action for social workers to address the systematic subjugation and pathologisation of people who have received 'mental health' diagnoses, to acknowledge that 'mental health care' can be oppressive and a form of social control, to engage with Mad movements and survivor activism, and to recognise the harms of medicalising discourses and othering practices. Mad Studies scholarship also offers highly generative opportunities for social work to engage with the critical knowledge, action, and grassroots advocacy of psychiatrised people, focused on the radical restructuring of 'mental health' paradigms, practices, and institutions, and 'devoted to the critique and transcendence of psy-centred ways of thinking, behaving, relating, and being' (Menzies, LeFrancois & Reaume, 2013, p.13). In this way, critical approaches also involve a critique of the dominance of biomedicine and coercive institutional practices, with a commitment to social change and building alliances with survivor movements.

Investigating Social Work Practices Fostering the Transformation of Mental Health Systems

This research set out to investigate contemporary social work practice focused on embodying, enacting, and promoting 'social change and development, social cohesion, and the empowerment and liberation of people… (following) principles of social justice, human rights, collective responsibility and respect for diversities' (IFSW, 2014) in the mental health field. As mental healthcare is dominated by a language of disorders and symptom management, and often experienced as a violation of personhood, social work seeks to bring a critical perspective to this field by identifying and addressing questions of inequality and agency (Bland et al., 2021). In our conversations, we were drawn to question: Who are positioned as the knowledge holders? Which knowledges are viewed as legitimate? When is social work supporting people? and When is it coercive, or not supportive at all? Seeking to address systemic transformation within the mental health care system is challenging. Social workers may face seemingly insurmountable challenges and constraints, and a seemingly enormous disconnect between social justice rhetoric and the messy realities of working within mental health organisations.

Such tensions are inherent to social work practice across a diverse array of fields, for example, child protection and disability sectors. However, it is highly concerning that critical practices are frequently absent from dominant conceptualisations of mental health social work (Brown, 2021). Social and organisational contexts characterised by rapidly increasing demand sit alongside rising pressure for accountability and efficiency (Hendrix et al., 2021). Market-oriented principles that categorise people according to 'risk factors' restrict the capacity of social workers to transform services and can lead to superficial or tokenistic approaches to upholding human rights. Working within such contexts can lead to substantial moral distress among social workers who want to make a difference (Tseris et al., 2024). Navigating these ongoing developments and pressures requires nimble, nuanced, and creative approaches. Consequently, it is important for social work to further develop ways of working collectively to respond to such challenges, and in solidarity with people with direct lived experiences, as it is not possible for individual social workers to transform mental health systems and paradigms on their own.

An additional complexity is a struggle within social work to articulate our practice, due to a knowledge base that is 'plural, ambiguous, situated and contested' (Daly et al., 2024, p.958). This is very different to the more static, positivist, and prescriptive knowledges that are drawn upon by almost all other mental health professions. As a response, we might try to mimic the approaches of other professionals to secure professional status and lean into certainty. We argue, however, that the rich and contextualised knowledge base of critical social work is something that is worth consolidating and fostering, as an alternative to diagnostic and therapeutic approaches, which require people to accept rigid, depoliticised, disempowering, and deficit-oriented responses to distress, crisis, and despair. Nevertheless, we seek to resist binary thinking such as macro/micro; critical/clinical; working with individuals/working with groups and communities (Bland et al., 2021; Brown, 2021). In fact, some of us deeply question the binary suggested by singling out a *critical social work*. Surely the social work 'principles of social justice, human rights, collective responsibility and respect for diversities' (IFSW, 2014) means social work is, by definition, 'critical'.

Moving beyond the constraints of a 'how to' guide, this book aims to explore examples of how social workers consider and apply a power analysis in the mental health field, across a range of diverse contexts, including roles within the public mental health system and private practice. *The setting or context in which we are situated does not need to define our practice.* For example, in a 'clinical' setting, in which we are expected to see individuals for mental health 'treatment' or 'therapy', if we choose to view our work through a 'clinical' lens, this may foreclose a lot of possibilities and constrain our opportunities to work in ways that acknowledge socio-political contexts and address social injustices. Our work may become focused on surveillance or assisting people to modify their behaviour and adjust to unfair social conditions. However, if we see mental health social work as always about addressing power and resisting notions of individual 'pathology', we may find generative opportunities to work in critically systemic ways and to address the politics of experience, despite the setting in which we are located (see Chap. 3 for a number of examples).

Our research also revealed the need to continue re-imagining 'mental health social work' in order to include roles outside 'mental health treatment', where social work practice might be involved in addressing the social drivers of distress, or supporting people to access the resources they need outside the mainstream mental health system. This includes advocacy, groupwork, and community work, which are often sidelined within a hierarchy of social work that privileges a 'clinical' role or identity. Through such processes, social workers can start to resist pathologising and deficit-based approaches, to instead enact insights from a power analysis and address the socio-political contexts of distress.

Writing the Book

Having acknowledged continued powerful influences on and within mental health systems, we explored social work practice in this field. Our aim was to look at how we not only **conceptualise and critically analyse** patterns of power in mental health, but how insights from this process have been **applied** in mental health social work practice. We were interested in the nuanced skills that social workers use in doing subversive work. We wanted to move beyond an acknowledgement of power, towards documenting the possibilities that exist for social workers to respond to injustices in everyday practice. Working 'clinically' in ways that focus on individuals, and step-by-step guidelines to 'treating' distress could seem an attractive approach to reducing complexity and offer certainty in the moment. On the other hand, we may become stuck in a structural analysis with no clear understanding of how critical theory and knowledge of social structures can be applied in our immediate interactions—we might even tell ourselves that 'we have no power in the system, and so there is no use in trying', deflecting from our accountability and ethical responsibilities as social workers to speak back to injustices. In contrast to these binary positions, our conversations revealed that theory and practice need not be so distanced from one another. Through collective analysis and connections with one another, an array of creative, critical practices was rendered visible (see Chaps. 2–5). Our discussions were not focused on developing formulaic principles, but rather, exploring nuanced skills and practices employed by critical social workers, over time, in responding to injustices and challenging diagnostic models. Importantly, the aim of the research was not to reach a place of certainty or comfort, acknowledging that 'there are no spaces of innocence in social work, and it is essential to attempt to remain attentive to relationships of power in each moment' (Barnhart, 2018). Moving beyond prescriptive and technocratic approaches to social work, we explore the possibilities that are present when social workers are attuned to power arrangements and contexts.

Overall, the research aimed to investigate how social work promotes emotional wellbeing and justice when employed in a mental health system that is permeated by exclusions, competition, pathologisation, violence, and coercion, due to the insidious domination of global capitalist, neoliberal, and biomedical ideas. Within this context, the research focus was refined to addressing the research question:

- How is social work enacting social justice in the mental health field?

The study was approved by Griffith University (GU Ref No: 2024/046).

Cooperative Inquiry

Cooperative Inquiry was chosen to guide the research given its capacity to support collective, deep, nuanced exploration of direct experience; its collaborative nature aligning well with social work values, and its functionality in researching social work innovations (for example, Whitaker et al., 2024). This method acknowledges and draws on experiential, presentational, propositional, and practical knowledges (Reason & Sohmer, 2019; Wooltorton & Reason, 2023). By acknowledging *experiential knowing,* the tacit knowledge of lived experience beyond direct articulation, we were invited to pause and reflect on the nuance of our experiences in practising mental health social work. In doing so, we were more aware that we were referring to, perhaps containing, this experience as *presentational knowing* through storytelling and artworks. We realised the map was not the territory. Instead, the map provided a language through which we could discuss the territory. We were familiar with *propositional knowing,* which involves drawing on concepts and ideas that assist in sense-making, such as theories of oppression and social work practice. However, by referring to these as a basis of comparison, rather than tailoring our *presentations* to fit theory, we aimed to avoid being blinkered by social work theory. Instead, we looked for interactions between theory and practice. Finally, this process enabled the identification, and collaborative generation and development of *practical knowing*, that is, the actions of mental health social work practice in embodying social justice, the ultimate focus of the study, captured in the chapters in this book.

In this study, the 'action' upon which we reflected was our experience of addressing social injustice in our mental health social work practice (Reason & Heron, 2013; Wooltorton & Reason, 2023). We engaged as co-researchers and co-subjects in critically reflective conversations via videoconferencing. Initially we met weekly, later fortnightly, throughout 2024, and into 2025. Our conversations were recorded and transcribed. Between meetings, two co-researchers, varying from week to week, met to manually code written transcripts of recordings of the meetings and identify and discuss emerging themes. Key themes were discussed at subsequent meetings, enabling collaborative, iterative analysis. Transcripts were also coded using N-Vivo software. Minutes, coded transcripts, the N-Vivo file, and working documents were available to co-researchers on a shared drive, facilitating access and further reflection.

The cooperative inquiry process involves several cycles of collective critical reflection on action (Reason & Heron, 2013; Wooltorton & Reason, 2023). In each cycle (Reason & Heron, 2013), we began by confirming the focus of the cycle of the inquiry before identifying and sharing representations of varying aspects of our individual experiences of fostering social justice in our mental health social work practice. We referred to preliminary analyses of the data to collectively, critically reflect on our representations, identifying findings. We drafted manuscripts discussing findings and, using collective critical reflection, these were reviewed to inform the development of chapters. Thus, the method itself was a political act as it deliberately enacted the collaborative and relational practices that we sought to acknowledge, examine, and articulate through this research.

Co-researchers

Co-researchers were invited to join on the basis of purposive and snowball sampling. We sought a research team covering metropolitan, regional, and rural social work practice experience across Australian eastern seaboard states; work experience in government, non-government, private practice, and academia; diverse lengths of practice experience; and commitment to critical reflective practice. Our team included:

Hollie Ballingall is a Yuin woman, raised on Dharawal Country, now living and working on Gadigal Land. She is a qualified Accredited Mental Health Social Worker who works from an anti-oppressive and de-colonial lens. She strongly believes that cultural, socioeconomic, and political nuances must be considered when developing wellness plans, particularly as it is these forces that can oppress or impede recovery.

Ashlea Borg is a critical social worker with experience working in community and government spaces. Ashlea is passionate about working with those impacted by systemic harms. She is also interested in ways that carceral systems are replicated by social services in particular social work settings. Ashlea aims to work in ways that are collaborative, trauma-informed, anti-oppressive and that celebrate the many ways individuals and communities have resisted social, economic, and political violence.

Binti Jones is a social worker with several years of experience in community services work across social housing, homelessness, mental health, and family services. She has worked in a range of clinical and leadership roles across government and non-government settings including inpatient and community-based mental health teams. She works as a casual academic with Southern Cross University with an interest in practice-based research in the field of mental health social work.

Alex Olsen has held a variety of positions in non-government, government mental health services and private practice working with children, young people and their families. Alex is passionate about inspiring connection—to self, to others, to the world—as a key tool in the fight against power, injustice, and systemic oppression.

Aimee Pitt is a social worker whose work has supported individuals, groups, and communities navigating distress and marginalisation. Aimee is driven to use their power as a social worker to critically reflect upon the systems and institutions in which they work. They have a passion for advocating for young people and LGBTQSB+ communities. They also have experience as a team leader in a large non-government organisation focused on youth mental health, and experience in community development.

Katherine Reid is a social work academic in Public Health and Social Work at the Queensland University of Technology. She has worked in a tertiary child and youth mental health community-based organisation and mental health policy contexts. Katherine is committed to make visible everyday forms of resistance that social workers enact in their mental health practice, to explore transformative possibilities, beyond the dominance of the biomedical model.

Lisa Thorpy retrained as a social worker following many years as an activist and community services worker. Since graduating she has worked in a range of clinical settings as well as in systems improvement positions both locally and at a statewide level. She is particularly interested in addressing people's experiences of and the system's responses to the intersections of marginalisation, trauma and violence in mental health services.

Emma Tseris is an academic in Social Work and Policy Studies at the University of Sydney. She has practice experience in mental health and has engaged in participatory action research aiming to challenge psychiatric oppression in women's lives. Emma comes to this project with a keen interest in disrupting social work's complicity with biomedical and coercive practices.

Louise Whitaker is a social work academic. Before teaching mental health social work at Southern Cross University, Australia, Louise practised in mental health, women's health, and legal services. Louise welcomes this project as an opportunity to recognise and resource transformative, sustainable mental health social work practice.

Demonstrating the limitations of the binary identities of 'professional' and 'client', as well as our social work identities, some of us also have experiences of receiving mental health services, and/or supporting friends and family members interfacing with the mental health system. We do not present our analysis as 'final' or 'complete', but as an emerging and continual process of learning.

Developing the Book Chapters

This book, and the chapters within it, is the product of cycles of inquiry. These cycles investigated: embodying social justice (January to March 2024); conceptualising mental health social work (March to May 2024); expanding the gaze (June to July 2024); direct practice foregrounding social justice in mental health (September to November 2024); and holding the line between transformation and complicity (February to March 2025). While topics were examined sequentially, the chapters were written concurrently. In cooperative inquiry, all co-researchers are co-authors. While cooperative inquiry often does not use pseudonyms, we adopt pseudonyms in Chaps. 2–6 to assist in de-identifying organisational details in the practice reflections shared. All information relating to clients and colleagues has been de-identified within the quotes.

In Chap. 2, we reveal a mosaic of possible conceptualisations of mental health social work revealing numerous implicit and co-existent influences on how we understand this practice. The mosaic is not intended to be prescriptive of content. Rather the image acknowledges the multiplicity of influences on how social work practice in this field might be conceptualised. In Chap. 3, we discuss direct practice centring lived experience while elevating socio-political contexts. In Chap. 4, we describe practices of resistance in response to coercive practices. In Chap. 5, we expand our gaze to working with community and navigating tensions in taking this approach in systems dominated by managerialism. Finally in Chap. 6, we explore how we have positioned ourselves to nurture capacity and capability for holding *the fine line between transformation and complicity*.

Conclusion

While social work brings a power analysis to the field of mental health, the context deters engagement in practices promoting social justice. Having highlighted these multiple contextual barriers, this chapter described the cooperative inquiry in which we engaged to explore mental health social work practice informed by an analysis of power. Our aim was not to articulate a set of practice guidelines—for example, communication skills that can be applied universally—as we took the position that critical practices in the mental health field cannot be reduced to applying a set of generic skills. Therefore, in the next chapter, we begin by mapping in more detail the contexts shaping how we conceptualise mental health social work. This project sought to bring careful attention to locating mental health social work within contexts of practice in order to investigate how practice influences, and is influenced by, practice contexts.

References

Bark, H., Dixon, J., & Laing, J. (2023). The professional identity of social workers in mental health services: A scoping review. *International Journal of Environmental Research and Public Health, 20*(11), 5947. https://doi.org/10.3390/ijerph20115947 [orca.cardiff.ac.uk]

Barnhart, M. (2018). Oppositional defiant disorder: The psy apparatuses and youth resistance. *Journal of Progressive Human Services, 29*(1), 6–27.

Becker-Blease, K. A. (2017). As the world becomes trauma–informed, work to do. *Journal of Trauma & Dissociation, 18*(2), 131–138.

Bland, R., Drake, G., & Drayton, J. (2021). *Social work practice in mental health: an introduction (3rd ed)*. Routledge.

Brown, C. (2020). Critical clinical social work: Theoretical and practical considerations. In C. Brown & J. McDonald (Eds.), *Critical clinical social work: Counter-storying for social justice* (pp. 16–58). Canadian Scholars' Press.

Brown, C. (2021). Critical clinical social work and the neoliberal constraints on social justice in mental health. *Research on Social Work Practice, 31*(6), 644–652.

Capra, F., & Luisi, P. L. (2016). *The systems view of life: A unifying vision*. Cambridge University Press.

Cohen, B. M. (2016). Psychiatric hegemony: A Marxist theory of mental illness. Palgrave Macmillan.

Daley, A., Costa, L., & Beresford, P. (Eds.). (2019). *Madness, violence, and power: A critical collection*. University of Toronto Press.

Daly, M., McCulloch, T., & Smith, M. (2024). The place of knowledge in constructing social work identity: Validating vagueness. *The British Journal of Social Work, 54*(3), 958–975.

Davies, J. (2021). *Sedated: How modern capitalism created our mental health crisis*. Atlantic Books.

Dawson, L., River, J., McCloughen, A., & Buus, N. (2020). 'Every single minute and hour is scrutinised': neoliberalism and Australian private mental health care. *Sociology of Health & Illness, 42*(2), 277–292.

Daya, I. (2022). Russian dolls and epistemic crypts: A lived experience reflection on epistemic injustice and psychiatric confinement. *Inc, 3*(2).

Department of Health. (2019) 'Reflections: Social work and mental health in Northern Ireland'. *Office of Social Service's Reflection Series, 3*, available online at https://www.health-ni.gov.uk/sites/default/files/publications/health/Reflections-3-Mental-Health-v4_0.pdf (last accessed May 18, 2023).

Dudgeon, P., Watson, M., & Holland, C. (2017). Trauma in the aboriginal and Torres Strait islander population. *Australian Clinical Psychologist, 3*(1), 1741.

Dudgeon, P. (2020). Decolonising psychology: Self-determination and social and emotional well-being. In A. Moreton-Robinson, C. Anderson, S. Larkin, B. Hokowitu, & L. Tuhiwai-Smith (Eds.), *The Routledge handbook of critical indigenous studies* (pp. 100–113). Taylor and Francis.

Foucault, M. (1978). The history of sexuality: Volume 1 – An introduction (R. Hurley, Trans.). Random House. (Original work published 1976).

Foucault, M. (1980). Power/knowledge: Selected interviews and other writings, 1972–1977 (C. Gordon, Ed.; C. Gordon, L. Marshall, J. Mepham, & K. Soper, Trans.). Harvester Press.

Frances, A. (2013). *Saving Normal an insider's revolt against out-of-control psychiatric diagnosis, DSM-5, big pharma, and the medicalization of ordinary life*. HarperCollins Publishers.

Francis, C. J., Johnson, A., & Wilson, R. L. (2022). The personal cost of repetitive mental health inquiries that fail to result in change. *Collegian, 29*(5), 728–737.

Fricker, M. (2007). *Epistemic injustice: Power and the ethics of knowing*. Oxford University Press.

Fullagar, S. (2018). Foucauldian theory. In B. M. Z. Cohen (Ed.), *Routledge international handbook of critical mental health* (pp. 39–45). Routledge.

Hendrix, E., Barusch, A., & Gringeri, C. (2021). Eats me alive! Social workers reflect on practice in neoliberal contexts. *Social Work Education, 40*(2), 161–173.

Helbich, M., & Jabr, S. (2022). A call for social justice and for a human rights approach with regard to mental health in the occupied Palestinian territories. *Health and Human Rights, 24*(2), 305.

Hersey, T. (2022). *Rest is resistance: A manifesto*. Hachette UK.

International Federation of Social Workers. (2014) *Global definition of social work*. Available online at https://www.ifsw.org/what-is-social-work/global-definition-of-social-work/

Jacob, J. D., Gagnon, M., Perron, A., & Canales, M. K. (2021). Revisiting the concept of othering: A structural analysis. *Advances in Nursing Science, 44*(4), 280–290.

Lemke, T. (2016). Foucault's hypothesis: From the critique of the juridico-discursive concept of power to an analytics of government. *Parrhesia, 9*, 18.

Manchester, R. (2015). Towards critical mental health social work: Learning from critical psychiatry and psychiatry survivors. *Critical and Radical Social Work, 3*(1), 149–154.

Maylea, C. H. (2017). A rejection of involuntary treatment in mental health social work. *Ethics and Social Welfare, 11*(4), 336–352.

Medina, J. (2013). *The epistemology of resistance: Gender and racial oppression, epistemic injustice, and the social imagination*. Oxford University Press.

Menzies, R., LeFrancois, B. A., & Reaume, G. (2013). Introducing mad studies. In B. A. LeFrançois, R. Menzies, & G. Reaume (Eds.), *Mad matters: A critical reader in Canadian mad studies. pp. 1-22*. Canadian Scholars' Press.

Milroy, H., Kashyap, S., Collova, J., Mitchell, M., Ryder, A., Cox, Z., et al. (2024). Walking together in friendship: Learning about cultural safety in mainstream mental health services through aboriginal participatory action research. *Australian & New Zealand Journal of Psychiatry, 58*(6), 498–505.

Mills, C. (2018). The mad are like savages and the savages are mad: psychopolitics and the coloniality of the psy. In B. M. Z. Cohen (Ed.), *Routledge international handbook of critical mental health* (pp. 205–212). Routledge.

Moncrieff, J. (2022). The political economy of the mental health system: A Marxist analysis. *Frontiers in Sociology, 6*, 771875.

Moreton-Robinson, A. (2015). *The white possessive: Property, power, and indigenous sovereignty*. University of Minnesota Press.

Morley, C., & Macfarlane, S. (2010). Repositioning social work in mental health: Challenges and opportunities for critical practice. *Critical Social Work, 11*(2), 46–59. https://doi.org/10.22329/csw.v11i2.5823

Muller, L. (2020). Preparing to work with aboriginal and Torres Strait islander peoples: Decolonisation for social work practice. In J. Maidment & R. Egan (Eds.), *Practice skills in social work and welfare* (pp. 84–100). Routledge.

Newcomb, M., & Venning, A. (2024). Defending discomfort: A critical social work case against trigger warnings. *Journal of Social Work Education*, 1–11.

Oute, J., & McPherson, S. (2023). *Conflict and antagonism within global psychiatry: A discourse analysis of organisational response to the UN reports on rights-based approaches to mental health* (pp. 1–22). Sociology of Health & Illness.

Pease, B. (2020). From evidence-based practice to critical knowledge in post-positivist social work. In B. Pease, J. Allan, & L. Briskman (Eds.), *Critical social work* (pp. 45–57). Routledge.

Poole, J. M., Jivraj, T., Arslanian, A., Bellows, K., Chiasson, S., Hakimy, H., Pasini, J., & Reid, J. (2012). Sanism, 'mental health', and social work/education: A review and call to action. *Intersectionalities: A Global Journal of Social Work Analysis, Research, Polity, and Practice, 1*, 20–36.

Reason, P., & Heron, J. (2013). Co-operative inquiry. In P. Reason & H. Bradbury (Eds.), *The SAGE handbook of action research: Participative inquiry and practice* (2nd ed., pp. 169–180). SAGE Publications.

Reason, P., & Sohmer, R. (2019). Practices of self and community: A participatory inquiry. In H. Bradbury (Ed.), *The SAGE handbook of participatory research and inquiry* (pp. 387–396). SAGE Publications. https://doi.org/10.4135/9781529704878

Reid, K., & Alford, J. (2023). Empowerment or holding the child responsible? An Australian recovery-oriented mental health policy analysis. *The British Journal of Social Work, 53*(5), 2860–2877.

Reid, K. (2023). *Who has naming rights? The framing of children's mental health issues in discursive therapy with their caregivers*. Child & Family Social Work.

Ross, D. (2020). Toward coercion free, trauma-informed care in Australian adult mental health services: Strategies for social workers. *Social Work in Mental Health, 18*(5), 536–553.

Ryan, J., & Ivelja, J. (2023). Indigenisation,(de) colonisation, and whiteness: Dismantling social work education. *Australian Social Work, 76*(3), 300–314.

Savaya, R., & Gardner, F. (2012). Critical reflection to identify gaps between espoused theory and theory-in-use. *Social Work, 57*(2), 145–154.

Sinclair, A., & Mahboub, L. (2024). Maddening post-qualitative inquiry: An exercise in collective (mad) theorising. *Qualitative Health Research, 34*(13), 1247–1260.

Slemon, A., Jenkins, E., & Bungay, V. (2017). Safety in psychiatric inpatient care: The impact of risk management culture on mental health nursing practice. *Nursing Inquiry, 24*(4), e12199.

Stark, C. (2018). The neoliberal ideology, its contradictions, the consequences and challenges for social work. *Ljetopis Socijalnog Rada [Annual of Social Work], 25*(1), 39–63.

Stone, K., McCusker, P., Davidson, G., & Vicary, S. (2021). An exploratory survey of mental health social work in Europe. *International Journal of Environmental Research and Public Health, 18*, 10462.

Tascon, S., & Gatwiri, K. (2020). Towards cultural humility: Theorising cultural competence as institutionalised whiteness. *Social Work & Policy Studies: Social Justice, Practice and Theory, 3*(1).

Tseris, E., Franks, S., & Hart, E. B. (2024). *Psychiatric oppression in women's lives*. Palgrave.

United Nations Human Rights Office of the High Commissioner. (2017). *World needs "revolution" in mental health care* https://www.ohchr.org/en/press-releases/2017/06/world-needs-revolution-mental-health-care-un-rights-expert?LangID=E&NewsID=21689

United Nations General Assembly Human Rights Council. (2017). *Report of the special rapporteur on the right of everyone to the enjoyment of the highest attainable standard of physical and mental health*. https://ap.ohchr.org/documents/dpage_e.aspx?si=A/HRC/35/21

van Noppen, C., Yassine, L., & Olcoń, K. (2024). Whiteness in our understanding of culture: A critical discourse analysis of the cultural responsivity practice frameworks in child protection. *Qualitative Social Work, 23*(6), 1008–1024.

Whitaker, L., Graeme-Cook, C., Jeffreys, J., Happell, B., Leach, M. & Vosz, M. (2024). Interweaving narratives of lived experience in mental health social work curriculum, Australian Social Work. https://doi.org/10.1080/0312407X.2023.2299924

Whitaker, L., Smith, F. L., Brasier, C., Petrakis, M., & Brophy, L. (2021). Engaging with transformative paradigms in mental health. *International Journal of Environmental Research and Public Health, 18*(18), 9504.

Wooltorton, S., & Reason, P. (2023). Experiential knowing with the more-than-human world. In P. White, R. Tytler, J. P. Ferguson, & J. Cripps Clark (Eds.), *Methodological Approaches to STEM Education Research* (Vol. 4, pp. 187–206). Cambridge Scholars Publishing. https://works.bepress.com/sandra-wooltorton/65/

World Health Organisation. (2025). *World health statistics 2025: Monitoring health for the SDGs, Sustainable Development Goals*. https://iris.who.int/bitstream/handle/10665/381418/9789240110496-eng.pdf?sequence=1

Wright, A., Gray, P., Selkirk, B., Hunt, C., & Wright, R. (2024). *Attachment and the (mis) apprehension of aboriginal children: epistemic violence in child welfare interventions* (pp. 1–25). Psychiatry.

Chapter 2
Power and Paradox in Mental Health Social Work: Mapping the Terrain

In this chapter, we map a mosaic of possible conceptualisations of social work practice within the mental health field in the Global North. This mosaic reveals the influences of multiple socio-political contexts on understandings of mental health social work. These influences render this area of practice highly complex and challenging, as social work is located within the very structures that it seeks to destabilise. Using a cooperative inquiry methodology and drawing on the voices of 9 women working together as co-researchers (see Chap. 1), our analysis seeks to draw attention to the political nature of mental health social work practice '*whether we recognise it or not*' (Barbie), including endeavours in '*putting things back together*' (Margaret) in ways that foster strength and justice. In this way, social work practice in the mental health field involves both close attention to power, points of resistance and opportunities to enact social change.

In addition to outlining various conceptualisations of mental health social work, we acknowledge the paradoxes associated with enacting social justice within oppressive socio-political contexts. The images we have included refer to these paradoxes. The chapter includes diverse discussions about grounding in Country, recognising White privilege and holding ourselves accountable, understanding social work's positioning in the capitalist system, navigating competing discourses, naming psychiatric violence, the personal is political, and recognising the beauty in acts of survivorship.

A Mosaic of Possibilities: Examining Conceptualisations of Mental Health Social Work

Social work's brief for 'promot(ing) social change and development, social cohesion, and the empowerment and liberation of people… (following) principles of social justice, human rights, collective responsibility and respect for diversities'

L. Whitaker et al., *Social Work in the Mental Health Field*, SpringerBriefs in Social Work, https://doi.org/10.1007/978-3-032-08306-7_2

(International Federation of Social Workers, 2014) hallmarks the profession's focus on the influences of social systems on well-being and the need for both systemic transformation and social change. While the identity of social work centres on a critical, political, and systemic understanding of distress and a brief for fostering social justice, such a conceptualisation may simplify, obscure, or minimise the paradoxical positioning of a profession engaged by a system, with a brief to change the system in which we are employed. This obliqueness might explain why many social workers do not take more opportunities to contest biomedical neoliberalism within the mental health field, instead accommodating diagnostic language and interventions that only focus on individuals conforming and adjusting to inequalities (Brown, 2021).

The mosaic of possibilities (as depicted in Fig. 2.1) maps the complex positioning of mental health social work identified in this research. It is a collective representation of findings from our exploration of social work within the mental health field. We use images intentionally as a way of moving past the limitations of intellectual engagement and the constraints of traditional text-based approaches to research, towards an embodied, experiential, and creative analysis of our

Fig. 2.1 Mosaic of the images referred to in this chapter including blank spaces

experiences in the mental health field. While the conceptualisations are discussed sequentially, there is no suggestion of priority or hierarchy. Nevertheless, as we write from unceded lands in the Australian context, we begin by honouring 'Grounding in Country' and 'Holding ourselves accountable'.

Grounding in Country

Alyssa is a proud Yuin woman who lives and works on unceded Dharawal Land and her image reflects how she looks after her own wellbeing. For Alyssa, as depicted in Fig. 2.2:

> *... the most important thing for my mental health is grounding in Country. I am a Saltwater woman, so for me, grounding in Country is connecting with the ocean, and I've always done that even since when I was very little. If I'm very dysregulated or feeling disconnected, if I go take a dip in the ocean, it centres me. Mental health is holistic. All health is holistic. For Mob, mental health cannot be separated from our communities and our Country. There's a well-being framework that's called the Social and Emotional Wellbeing Framework and it's got seven aspects connecting to culture, connecting to Country, family and kinship, mind and emotions, body (Dudgeon et al., 2014). All my work in this field is focused on this holistic way of caring for people. If you're not addressing your connection to each of those domains, your mental health is going to be out of whack.*

In contrast, dominant understandings of 'mental health' are steeped in a White, Western, and medicalised paradigm. This was noted by Scarlett who stated:

Fig. 2.2 'Cronulla'. Image credit: Author's own photograph

> The concept of mental health is based on a more individual notion that we can be mentally well by doing these individual strategies. This doesn't fit with the notion of wellbeing that is only possible through connection to Country, people and to culture.

Alyssa explained the importance of changing the entire basis of the way we look at mental health to properly decolonise because as she explains '*the entire basis of mental health diagnosis and treatment needs to change because it is fundamentally built off the DSM and is written by people who thought escaping slavery was an illness*'. Decolonising social work practice in mental health does not somehow occur through attending cultural safety training alone (Tujague & Ryan, 2021). Alyssa described:

> I walk into public service spaces and everyone's talking about strength-based, person-centred & trauma informed approaches saying 'We want to make sure that we're culturally appropriate. We want to do cultural safety training'. But then at the core of their work, they're all still very Westernised, White and power focused.

Alyssa described how various state governments in Australia, such as New South Wales, have implemented policies and procedures to include social and emotional well-being frameworks, and this is the preferred way of working with Aboriginal people. She pointed out how these developments are positive '*but it doesn't actually feed down to the frontline level, because ultimately, psychiatrists are in charge of decisions and psychiatrists are trained in a medical model that's deficit-based*'. Alyssa highlighted that:

> There's a real cognitive dissonance in having [mental health staff] tell you to your face, 'we really want to change systems. We want to do better for Aboriginal people' and then not actually changing the system in any meaningful way which would benefit Aboriginal people's wellbeing. That's the continuing colonial violence.

While recognising past complex and intergenerational trauma caused by colonisation is important (Atkinson & Atkinson, 2017), we discussed how essential is it to acknowledge the ongoing trauma that First Nations communities experience. For example, the 2022 referendum in Australia that gave the public a vote on whether First Nations people should have a Voice to Parliament, increased the prevalence of racism towards First Nations communities. The negative result of the referendum was dehumanising, reinforcing the distress for First Nations peoples in Australia. Alyssa questioned: '*How do you recover from historical trauma when you have current trauma being enacted to you*?' She explained:

> The core teaching of trauma theory is that you can't heal from trauma if you're not in a safe environment. Aboriginal people are not in a safe environment in this country. It also speaks to the failings of the very individualised nature of therapy. Even if you were going to treat someone using a trauma-based intervention, you can't do it properly if you acknowledge what we're experiencing in this country, which is very real current trauma. There is so much focus on intergenerational trauma and the effects that that has had on mental health of our people, and rightfully so, but no one talks about the current real trauma that we experience. And you cannot heal from trauma if you are currently in trauma, and so you're setting

> people up to fail. This then feeds into, 'You're not doing the work. You are treatment resistant'. It absolves the system of responsibility.

In brief, Indigenous people continue to be distressed by systems perpetuating colonial violence and personalised solutions to resolving distress. Paradoxically, accepting the support available, inadequate as it may be, requires acceptance of potentially depoliticised, individualised understandings of distress, whereas refusing 'treatment' is pathologised by mental health workers and incorporated into the individualised 'diagnosis'.

Holding Ourselves Accountable: White Supremacy, Colonisation, and Racism

The image of a crown reflects calls for recognition of colonial violence and its presence within the Australian mental health system (see Fig. 2.3). A costume crown was chosen, to demonstrate the constructed nature of colonial power, and the ways in which White supremacy should not be accepted but can and should be both identified and challenged in everyday social work practice. Recognising the multiple invitations to White comfort (Walter & Baltra-Ulloa, 2019), it is crucial that we do not ignore or minimise the impacts of Whiteness on our understandings and practices. Instead, we are all accountable, as noted by Frankie:

> I want to be holding myself accountable in this space, because otherwise I think we can step towards speaking about Aboriginal people and culture as 'the Other', when the viewpoint that I can write from is being a White worker, and how that poses challenges in the field. And how racism, and the racist structures that we work in, impact upon our ability to support all people, and in particular, First Nations people. I think it's a from a more ethical standpoint for me to write about Whiteness, the way that I experience it in the work, and the way that it might have caused harm to others. I've been lucky to have supervisors who, have challenged me around my colonial perspective, my Whiteness and maybe how that might be impeding on a relationship with somebody, or might be constricting my viewpoint, or how I might be excluding the views of others because of the White lens that I'm seeing things through.

It is important that non-Indigenous workers consider how they might leverage their privilege in ways that will be useful, in solidarity with First Nations people and communities, without becoming co-opted into colonial ways of thinking and acting. This reflection raises a paradox relating to the ways in which critical social workers are positioned within the mental health system. Despite an ethical commitment to undoing and reducing violence, this ethical stance is enacted within the very systems that are continuing to perpetrate harm against First Nations people and communities.

Fig. 2.3 A toy crown placed upon children's tulle costume skirts. Image credit: Author's own photograph

Serving Systems?: Mental Health Social Work as a Product of the Global Capitalist Arrangements That It Seeks to Resist and Influence

Like a cluster of water plants within a complex eco-system of rivers (see Fig. 2.4), clouds, and rain, Beatrice reflected on mental health social work as a product of the very global capitalism arrangements that it seeks to resist and influence. This raises important questions about the inherent paradoxes that play out when social workers espouse social justice values in mental health settings, while at the same time benefiting from the injustices of current capitalist arrangements. In addition to evoking a sense of scale, this metaphor raises questions about the place of the profession within existing oppressive global systems.

Fig. 2.4 Ross River, Townsville, Australia. Image credit: Author's own photograph

By addressing distress, and thereby bolstering economic and workforce capacity, is mental health social work engaged in mopping up the fall-out of a system founded on environmental degradation, greed and competition, and inherent inequality? This view acknowledges how complex systems, such as an eco-system revealed in a river of global capitalism, self-perpetuate and how then social work is potentially positioned, alongside the 'opiate of the masses', as deeply embedded within systems and political structures. By seeking to improve and safeguard social wellbeing—encompassing quality of relationships and sense of belonging; choice and control and having purpose and meaning in life as well as feeling safe and secure (Department of Health, 2019)—is mental health social work simply engaged in perpetuating current social systems? Alternatively, is the enticement from public to private mental health social work practice (Martin, 2013), with its promise of autonomy and creativity, not also evidence of perpetuating a capitalist approach? (Papadopoulos & Maylea, 2020). This view and these examples reveal a fundamental contradiction in espousing systemic and social change, while being engaged in humanising the existing care system and thus ensuring its continued role within global capitalism (Davies 2021).

By naming this fundamental paradox, that social work is functioning within a system perpetuating global capitalism while articulating principles of social justice undermined by global capitalism, we sought to acknowledge social work holds a *'possibly overwhelming [understanding] that hierarchy is power'* (Margaret). Is the challenge: *'if you're getting paid by the system, and your wage is funding your family holiday, then you are a part of the system'* (Scarlett). Sarah highlighted this is *'the politics'* that social work navigates, *'in refusing to turn away from that reality, which is a pretty tough reality, that all of us work or have worked in a system which is in many ways underpinned by harm and coercion'*. As Barbie said:

> When you're paid by patriarchy, you are definitely compromised but you're choosing to work within patriarchy. It's the old reform/revolution dichotomy. You're choosing to work in there, but it doesn't necessarily mean that you're working for them. You can actually be working to dismantle… But then I go back to that quote: 'the master's tools will never dismantle the master's house' (Lorde, 2018).

The situation need not be so bleak. A both/and view conceptualises mental health social work as humanising the system while changing it. Perhaps the inclusion of 'rights-based' practice in a recent European review of the distinctive contribution of social work in this field is indicative of a both/and approach (Stone et al., 2021), whereby mental health social work is conceptualised as utilising holistic, social, and rights-based models of mental health contrasting with medicalised approaches; a practice focused on empowerment, strengths-based and recovery approaches; and an understanding of the social impact of mental distress and associated questions of stigma and discrimination (Stone et al., 2021). Manchester (2015) describes the need for social work to end an 'us and them' mentality, by truly listening to and learning from the expertise of those who have been on the receiving end of services, so that we do not accept and replicate the status quo agendas of mental health systems. This can support social work to move past an agenda that seeks to merely improve rather than replace coercive systems, instead working towards changes that aim to dismantle oppressive structures and create lasting alternatives (Roper et al., 2023).

As social workers, we are attuned to the connections between harmful practices occurring within contemporary healthcare and their entanglement in broader managerialist regimes and global capitalist relations. Paradoxically, *'the reasons why it's so difficult for social workers to work in, say, a public mental health setting, where there are coercive practices, is also why it's really important for social workers to be in those settings and to… be able to provide a different perspective'* (Iris). As Barbie said, *'Akin to our approach to generating knowledge in this research project, a collective response is needed in mental health social work, to subvert neoliberal logics and to move from a sense of individual overwhelm and powerlessness as a "lone" practitioner, toward the possibilities of transformative practices'*.

Navigating a Spider's Web of Competing Discourses

The image of a spider's web signified for Scarlett mental health social workers communicating across competing discourses of mental health (see Fig. 2.5). Scarlett explained, *'recovery discourses espouse person-centred care to ensure that the person is setting their own goals for their recovery. Yet, the medical system I was*

Fig. 2.5 Colour photograph of a large spider's web. *Image credit: Author's own photograph*

working in required me to assess, diagnose and develop an individual treatment plan which often omitted children and young people's voices…' As Scarlett said:

> Spider webs are sticky … which illustrates how we can get inducted into medicalised and psychologised language informed by dominant psychiatric discourses, which can shape the way we think about the people we work with.

As a group we repeatedly questioned the politics of who gets to name what is occurring for a person, within the context of a biomedical hierarchy, where diagnostic formulations can overshadow lived experience understandings (Fricker, 2007; Reid, 2024). As Beatrice explained, *'this brief mapping of the terrain reveals the fact that different knowledges really dominate the way that we think'*. We discussed that once there is a diagnosis *'it's so controlling of the narrative'* (Barbie). Barbie described how you can see the *'narrative being created, building around her distress, but they're not calling it distress. They're calling it her Borderline Personality Disorder and self-harm'*. Iris explained:

> How a diagnosis can impact a person in their interactions, not only with their day-to-day life and their family, but also with other systems they may come in contact with. We often see a diagnosis in the mental health field as something that would benefit a person, by giving them more understanding of themselves, what's going on for them and what they're experiencing, but it can have quite significant implications as well.

Frankie further explained some of these implications by stating, *the diagnosis can be weaponised against people, particularly women, in the court system. A prime example is where the solicitors say, 'give me a list of every diagnosis she has'*. Our discussions highlighted the ways in which social work is cognisant of these implications and aims to navigate these injustices within systems.

The role diagnosis plays in sometimes enabling people to access funding is a further example of the insidious influence of language. Iris explained that the person may receive more support when a diagnosis is provided to a funding organisation. She described how this is done:

> Without of an acknowledgement of what the implications could be for that person individually in receiving that diagnosis and what that might mean for their family and their interactions with other systems.

Cassidy highlighted how diagnosis is the dominant discourse in mental health, limiting other explanations and frameworks of understanding:

> Diagnosis is often the currency that operates as a gatekeeper within our mental health and our support systems. Once someone has a diagnosis, it becomes less about what it means to them and their lived experience, and more about what it means to the systems that are meant to be supporting them.

We acknowledged how *we can have the best of intentions to try to join with the client, but how quickly we can fall into individualised language, particularly if the client is bringing that language like they have, maybe been a part of the mental health system for a while and have taken on board a medicalised way of understanding themselves and their identity* (Scarlett).

This view of mental health social work and an interrogation of diagnostic language recognises the 'unique and vital role in challenging simplistic, depoliticised individualising constructions of mental health and illness, and in advancing contextualised and holistic understandings of people's experiences' (Morley & Macfarlane, 2010, p.46). In 2008, Canadian colleagues articulated seven key principles of anti-oppressive mental health social work practice. They involved: inviting service users as full participants; respectful, egalitarian, empowering language; actively deconstructing the medical model with service users and their families and encouraging alternative healing perspectives; just working relationships; promoting education; embracing cultural diversity and strengths; and promoting principles of social justice (Larson, 2008). Referring to epistemic justice, Johnstone (2021) argues for relational social work practice grounded in empathic, active listening, challenging the silencing of lived experience and fostering personal agency, connectedness, and rebuilding positive identities. Brown (2021) discusses a critical approach to 'clinical' practice, which is centred on a socio-political analysis of mental health and aims to resist the co-option of social work into biomedical approaches. Nevertheless, as Cassidy said:

> I think that we have a tendency to get stuck on language and think that if we change language, we're changing politics and culture. But when we're working within and against violent systems, it's easy to forget how adaptable these systems are to resistance. So, although language is important because of what it represents politically, culturally and on an individual level, we can get stuck on it.

These reflections demonstrate the paradox at work, where social work promotes the transformation of language in the mental health field, and yet 'recovery-oriented' and 'strengths-based' ways of working can become co-opted by dominant biomedical discourses, leaving the hierarchy of knowledge unchallenged and silencing socio-political and lived experience knowledges.

Corridor: We May Have Impressive Words and Fancy Practice Guidelines, but People Are Still Experiencing the Service as Really Scary and as a Power-Over Approach

The image of an office corridor reminded Sarah of entrenched and persistent coercive practices in mental health systems, which can become so normalised that power relations can become concealed (see Fig. 2.6). As she said: 'W*e are socialised into wherever we're working and can start to not notice things. We might not notice the oppressive nature of our workplace over time'*. It is, therefore, necessary to consider how we might ensure ongoing accountability in our work, when we are located in systems that are enacting harm in the name of 'care'. This includes reflecting on the kinds of knowledges that we are drawing upon in the mental health field. While it is common for social workers to feel pressure to adopt 'clinical' ways of knowing (Brown, 2021), it is important that social workers refuse the persistent invitations to draw on forms of knowledge that enhance professional power and justify coercive practices (Chapman, 2014).

Within what we acknowledged was at times an *'exceptionally violent system'* (Barbie), mental health social work can adopt:

> A simplistic story that as a profession we work in an empowering way with the folks we work with. I think that's the intention, but then we join these systems that enact different forms of oppression and coercion. It's often difficult for us to acknowledge that there are forms of power that we are complicit in (Cassidy).

Thus, it is not just the nature of the system that needs exploration but also *'the stories that we tell each other; on the one hand, that we have no power to enact any change within hierarchical multidisciplinary teams; and on the other hand, that simply re-naming practices as 'trauma-informed' is sufficiently emancipatory. This binary thinking requires examination so that we can find possibilities to think and act differently'* (Sarah). In the contemporary context, it is noteworthy that it can be

Fig. 2.6 A narrow corridor, leading to a closed door. Image credit: Author's own photograph

difficult for psychiatric violence to be named, let alone addressed (Daley et al., 2019). Barbie reminded us by *'naming the unnameable, there are opportunities for everyday acts of subversion and resistance'*.

The corridor represents the risks, harms, and institutional violence that people experience in accessing mental health services. Conversely, the potential for a gentle and non-coercive space behind the door suggests *'pockets of subversiveness within institutions'* (Barbie). From this perspective, we can see mental health social work as a site of action, potentially creating spaces of resistance, to embody approaches that involve *'thinking and doing otherwise'* (Sarah). We also reflected on how as individual social workers who are attempting to enact critical practices, we can be *'connected through this process of cooperative inquiry'* (Barbie). This demonstrates the generative value of connections between social workers with shared ethical perspectives to develop solidarity and collective strategies for resistance. Through collaborative conversations that interrogate the paradox of holding onto a social justice perspective and trying to enact change while being employed within oppressive systems, critical mental health social work can start to consider points of resistance. Nevertheless, at the same time, social workers need to engage with the uncomfortable reality that *'there is sometimes a fine line between transformation and complicity'* (Sarah).

This image sparked discussion about mental health social work's brief for engaging in systemic transformations based on *'an expansive and uncompromising understanding of what it might mean to really transform the paradigm'* (Sarah). For Sarah, the generic office corridor, *'made me think about the sorts of "reforms" that happen in mental health spaces that unfortunately are often quite surface level, because we're not getting to the heart of oppression and coercion'* (Sarah). This image also reminded us of the influence of the physical environment on wellbeing, and how clinical spaces reflect and perpetuate a dominant biomedical paradigm, which is based upon separating people from their social contexts and communities. As Scarlett asked, *'How is it possible for services to support wellness and when the services are so disconnected from Country and nature? How do we incorporate both the cognitive and the body?'* Navigating this complexity might involve a *'tricky space of trying to find more creative ways'* (Margaret). This raises important questions about how much agency social workers have within the mainstream mental health system, to not only adopt a socio-political analysis of mental health, but to find ways for this analysis to influence practice.

Kintsugi: There's Something About the Strength of Putting Things Back Together That Can Make It More Than the Whole Before

Referring to the image of a kintsugi pot (Fig. 2.7), Margaret invited a reflection:

> When we have experiences of trauma, one of the losses is the capacity to be joyful and to be able to create. Because creativity is so closely linked to playfulness, when children experience trauma, it can take away their ability to play. Play is how we make sense of the world so finding ways for children to be able to play and experience joy is a key part of healing.

This particular cup, recreated using a Japanese art form that involves putting broken pieces back together with glue, signifies the *'capacity for joy and creativity ... that trauma takes away... [including the] trauma that they experienced in navigating all of the systems'*. This art form reveals the *'strength of putting things back together'* (Margaret) and how *'a broken cup put back together again can actually be more beautiful than it was before'* (Beatrice). At the same time:

> The paradox of the kintsugi pot is evident. There appears to be ever-increasing cultural norms of 'post-traumatic growth', that there is opportunity for growth even from the most challenging circumstances—'that which doesn't kill me makes me stronger'. This context places responsibility on the individual to not only survive adversity, pain and suffering but to develop 'internal strength'. It could be argued that this further perpetuates deficit-focused

Fig. 2.7 A broken jar glued back together. Image credit: Blue and gold pot, Author's own photograph

> assumptions—'what is wrong with this individual, that they haven't been able to grow?' (Margaret)

Considering this pot evoked multiple reflections about mental health social work. Firstly, in addition to not turning away from people's direct experiences of suffering, by distancing through diagnostic categorisation, mental health social work can acknowledge both the substantial impacts of injustices and the myriad ways in which people resist oppression. Further, notions of individual 'brokenness' should be challenged and re-positioned as systemic rather than individual failures, and seeing the beauty in acts of survivorship can inform hopeful systemic reconfiguration. As Sarah said: *'actually, people have the solutions. That really changes what you're doing in the work, getting past this idea that we're there to eliminate so-called symptoms'*. Secondly, the pot evoked ideas about making space for distress in mental health social work; making sure to avoid a position of 'expertise' or a 'fixing' approach, and instead walking in solidarity and partnership with people experiencing and resisting injustices. Thirdly, this pot recalls joy to mental health social work practice. As Sarah said: *'people deserve to have meaningful, joyful lives'*. Scarlett reminded us of the joy of creative ways of working even though *'the systems that we work in can be so … challenging for young people, children and workers alike (but obviously in different ways), [we] … find ways to hold those creative ways of working'*. Margaret confirmed, *'That's what has been sustaining for me in my practice has been working in teams that really value joy and creativity'*.

Like others, this metaphor for mental health social work also revealed paradoxes. As Margaret said:

> The value of playfulness and joy as a way to mitigate suffering has been present in some workplaces I have been part of and in hindsight, I wonder if the focus on the 'the shiny and gold' has led to ideas that we as workers should cope and be joyful in the face of suffering. I became so conscious of not infecting my colleagues with my growing sense of unease and rage about the injustices experienced by my clients and their families because I was worried that I would be perceived as not coping or experiencing burnout. Does this mirror the experience of clients who are told they are 'mentally unwell' or have a 'personality disorder' when they show the force of their rage?

In summary:

> The art of kintsugi perturbs the prevailing notion in our capitalist society that things and people are infinitely replaceable… However, if we see the kintsugi pot as representative of the broken-ness of the systems in which we operate and more broadly, ideas of capitalism and neoliberalism—in this telling, maybe the glitter and sparkles is the work that we do as social workers to navigate these systems. But does adding glue, glitter and sparkles make us complicit in hiding the broken-ness of the social structures?

Personal Is Political: Everything That We Do Is Political … Whether We Recognise It or Not

Inspired by a 1980s feminist slogan, Barbie reminded us *'everything that we do is political'*. The 'personal is political' slogan has referred to the performativity and social construction of gender, whereas Barbie referred to the image (see Fig. 2.8) to examine political influences, as illustrated with a story of:

> Walking to the beach with my grandsons and one of them wanted to run over the sand dunes … It gave me the opportunity to start to talk to him about our responsibility as human beings on the land and when I asked him what he knew about that, about litter. … made me think about our Western culture and about how to manage litter, but we're still not actually taught about not making litter. And so to me, that's a really great example of how the personal is political. So that I could talk to him about why we don't make litter and about our responsibility to look after the land and how he is an individual can actually contribute to that wider idea of caring for the land.

Thus, the personal, and by implication the professional, have impacts *'whether we recognise it or not. … Being blind to it … [is actually] positioning yourself as centre … [and] othering'* (Barbie).

Our discussions made explicit the way we conceptualise our work and the connection between analysis and practice. In bringing a power analysis, we discussed how the 'personal' is very much 'political' when working with individuals in a 'clinical' context. We explicitly identified that people's experiences of distress are

Fig. 2.8 Fist raised in solidarity. Image credit: 'Raised fist png illustration, transparent', retrieved from rawpixel.com (Reproduced from rawpixel.com. Some modification was made. https://www.rawpixel.com/image/7613787/png-hand-vintage, licensed under the terms of CC0 1.0 Universal (https://creativecommons.org/publicdomain/zero/1.0/deed.en))

in response to key events such as lived experiences of injustice and violence in their everyday lives. Refusing the language of 'illness' and exploring more expansive understandings of human experiences was important for our collective, as Scarlett described:

> I'm drawn to the phrase 'distress' because I think it immediately shines the light onto that broader context and that this is a reaction to a situation and, not some sort of example of an individual issue, failing or lack of coping.

There are many other possible words, including but not limited to, suffering, fear, despair, overwhelm, and madness—a term used by many psychiatrised people to reclaim a previously pejorative term. A key challenge when working in biomedical clinical settings is how we, as social workers, are professionally inducted into focusing on the presenting 'mental health concerns' and individual symptoms, to assess and deliver 'evidence-based' interventions. This is based on a narrow perspective on what counts as evidence (Pease, 2020). In contrast, a critical perspective recognises that distress co-occurs 'with marginalisation, oppression and inequity' (Brown, 2021, p. 645). This was important to acknowledge, to avoid individualising, decontextualising, and pathologising experiences of distress. As noted by Scarlett:

> I think individualised concepts such as 'mental health concerns' or 'issues' or 'diagnosis' can eradicate or make invisible the context of a person's life.

Beatrice further explained:

> Domestic violence might actually impact on the person's situation and yet, and when we're looking from a biomedical view, we're only looking at the mental health symptoms and the person and not necessarily taking the context into account.

Scarlett also described how:

> Depending on the language we use, can individualise the experience. For example, if a young person's experience is labelled as 'anxiety' without any contextualising or looking at whether their response is in relation to homophobia or some other form of oppression, we're missing the cause of the person's distress and we're just loading up that responsibility on to the individual to do their CBT [cognitive behavioural therapy] sessions and better manage their 'anxiety' whilst leaving the status quo unchallenged.

Our approach to working with individuals and communities involves making visible these enduring social structures that perpetuate distress, and the ways in which the language of 'illness' conceals such structures. For example, Barbie explained the possibilities that can be opened up when we depart from a diagnostic approach:

> If we talk about distress, then the people, the other people around them, it evokes a sense of caring, rather than judgement.

Within the biomedical model, 'evidence-based' knowledge is prioritised over knowledge derived from lived experience. As Alyssa explains, *'I'm constantly having to push back on the evidence-based thing because I currently work in the hospital system'*. Because this hierarchy of knowledge can subjugate lived experience expertise, we need to be intentional and thoughtful as to how to centre and elevate lived experience.

The 'personal is political' slogan of the critical feminist movement of the 1980s remains relevant. *'Underpinned by feminist theory, it highlights notions of power'* (Barbie). This visual representation recognises the political nature and impact of personal or professional actions when the collective nature of 'the personal is political' is considered. The image spoke to solidarity across diversity, capturing *'the power of the collective standing united with all of our different intersectionalities. Women, people of colour and queer people have to stand together'* (Barbie). The fist is a symbol of collective struggle and solidarity even though it is an individual fist. So, this image also speaks to the power of collectivism, of *'solidarity, the collective, … breaking down false social boundaries, that we stand individually and professionally… where difference between us is constructed'* (Barbie). By acknowledging its deeply political nature, this image prompts questions about how mental health social work upholds its contribution to social justice while enacting solidarity alongside diverse collectives of people with lived experience, in comparison to an 'us' and 'them' approach. Where the 'spider's web' reminds of the stickiness of dominant languages, this image brings attention to relationships, positionality, and power in mental health social work and *'the way in which the macro and the micro are connected'* (Barbie). Barbie also recalled how *'our fights for social justice are not exclusive, that this isn't a single issue for one group or another'*. Thus, *'coming together with marginalised groups… creates more power overall as … the people united will never be defeated….'* (Barbie). Paradoxically, holding common ground can also mean the contribution of mental health social work is less visible in comparison to than other mental health workers with more 'bounded' roles, so that striving to do ourselves out of a job might indeed be achieved—not because the injustices have been resolved, but due to a neoliberal cost-cutting agenda that does not see the 'value' of social work (Daly et al., 2024). This reveals the tension in mental health social work between resisting rigid and measurable certainties and de-centring professional knowledge, while aiming to articulate and refine the profession's skills and knowledge in enacting social justice.

Navigating Paradoxes of Being Within Systems While Promoting Their Transformation

In this chapter, we have explored the myriad ways in which mental health social work is positioned. At its heart, social work navigates paradoxes emerging from being employed within a system that it is seeking to transform. These paradoxes include offering 'treatment' prescribed by colonisers for the distress caused by perpetual colonisation; performing language and support strategies that reinforce individualised conceptualisations of distress; perpetuating individualised responsibility for surviving adversity, pain, suffering and developing 'internal strength', when acknowledging the courage and strength of individuals in navigating adversity; and articulating principles of social justice while benefiting from global capitalism. In brief, these paradoxes emerge from holding a social justice perspective informing the enactment of change while being employed within oppressive systems. Thus, in addition to the personal being political, the political infiltrates the enactment of social work practice. How might we 'not turn away' from these paradoxes and continue to uphold principles of the profession while working in mental health? Like water plants swept to the side by the currents of the river, clustered by the bank, this inquiry has provided the opportunity for 'naming the unnameable' with colleagues, acknowledging the limitations of analysis and critique, leading to opportunities to explore critical practices in everyday social work settings.

Critical systems theory provided a foundation for recognising and understanding the complexity of mental health systems. As Iris said: '*social workers are kind of unique in a way in their ability to be able to see the broader picture and the person's interactions with other systems and other parts of their life*'. In this way, social work can be seen as a form of *applied* social justice—weaving the personal and the political and moving between big-picture systemic analysis and the nuances of lived experience. We confirmed the consistent navigation of power and the dominance of pathologising and managerial discourses in everyday social work practice. Critical social work practice in the mental health field is therefore not simply about learning de-contextualised skills (for example, active listening, 'case' management and advocacy), but requires a more complex embodiment of a social justice perspective in moment-to-moment interactions with people, families, communities, and multidisciplinary teams. Stepping beyond the comfort of merely critiquing the current system, our cooperative inquiry found that social workers can and do find ways to navigate biomedical terrain in order to make space for more liberatory practices. The details of how we have grappled with achieving this in practice are the focus of the following three chapters (Chap. 3, 4, and 5).

References

Atkinson & Atkinson. (2017). A healing foundation for Aboriginal community development. In Kickett-Tucker, C., Bessarab, D., Coffin, J. & Wright, M. (Eds.). *Mia Mia Aboriginal community development: Fostering cultural security* (pp. 110–127).

Brown, C. (2021). Critical clinical social work and the neoliberal constraints on social justice in mental health. *Research on Social Work Practice, 31*(6), 644–652.

Chapman, C. (2014). Becoming perpetrator: How I came to accept restraining and confining disabled aboriginal children. In B. Burstow, B. A. LeFrancois, & S. Diamond (Eds.), *Psychiatry disrupted: Theorizing resistance and crafting the (R)evolution* (pp. 16–33). McGill-Queen's University Press.

Daley, A., Costa, L., & Beresford, P. (2019). Introduction. In A. Daley, L. Costa, & P. Beresford (Eds.), *Madness, violence, and power: A critical collection* (pp. 3–20). University of Toronto Press.

Daly, M., McCulloch, T., & Smith, M. (2024). The place of knowledge in constructing social work identity: Validating vagueness. *The British Journal of Social Work, 54*(3), 958–975.

Davies, J. (2021). *Sedated: How modern capitalism created our mental health crisis*. Atlantic Books.

Department of Health. (2019). 'Reflections: Social work and mental health in Northern Ireland', *Office of Social Service's reflection series,* 3. https://www.health-ni.gov.uk/sites/default/files/publications/health/Reflections-3-Mental-Health-v4_0.pdf.

Dudgeon, P., Rickwood, D., Garvey, D., & Gridley, H. (2014). A history of indigenous psychology. In P. Dudgeon, H. Milroy, & R. Walker (Eds.), *Working together: Aboriginal and Torres Strait islander mental health and wellbeing principles and practice* (pp. 39–54). Commonwealth of Australia.

Fricker, M. (2007). *Epistemic injustice: Power and the ethics of knowing*. Oxford University Press.

Lorde, A. (2018). *The master's tools will never dismantle the master's house*. Penguin Classics.

International Federation of Social Workers. (2014). *Global definition of social work*. Available online at https://www.ifsw.org/what-is-social-work/global-definition-of-social-work/

Johnstone, M. (2021). Centering social justice in mental health practice: Epistemic justice and social work practice. *Research on Social Work Practice, 31*(6), 634–643.

Larson, G. (2008). Anti-oppressive practice in mental health. *Journal of Progressive Human Services, 19*(1), 39–54.

Manchester, R. (2015). Towards critical mental health social work: Learning from critical psychiatry and psychiatry survivors. *Critical and Radical Social Work, 3*(1), 149–154.

Martin, J. (2013). Accredited mental health social work in Australia: A reality check. *Australian Social Work, 66*(2), 279–296.

Morley, C., & Macfarlane, S. (2010). Repositioning social work in mental health: Challenges and opportunities for critical practice. *Critical Social Work, 11*(2), 46–59.

Papadopoulos, A., & Maylea, C. (2020). Medicare funded mental health social work: Better access to what? *Australian Social Work, 73*(2), 137–148.

Pease, B. (2020). From evidence-based practice to critical knowledge in post-positivist social work. In J. Allan, L. Briskman, & B. Pease (Eds.), *Critical social work* (pp. 45–57). Routledge.

Reid, K. (2024). Who has naming rights? The framing of children's mental health issues in discursive therapy with their caregivers. *Child and Family Social Work, 29*(1), 48–57.

Roper, C., Edan, V., Joffee-Kohn, N., Hamilton, B. & Gooding, P. (2023). *Abolitionist perspectives: Project report.* https://healthsciences.unimelb.edu.au/__data/assets/pdf_file/0007/5063497/CMHN_Abolition_Perspectives_Report.pdf

Stone, K., McCusker, P., Davidson, G., & Vicary, S. (2021). An exploratory survey of mental health social work in Europe. *International Journal of Environmental Research and Public Health, 18*(19), 1–16.

Tujague, N. A., & Ryan, K. L. (2021). Ticking the box of 'cultural safety' is not enough: Why trauma-informed practice is critical to indigenous healing. *Rural and Remote Health, 21*(3), 1–5.

Walter, M., & Baltra-Ulloa, A. J. (2019). Australian social work is white. In B. Bennett & S. Green (Eds.), *Our voices: Aboriginal social work* (pp. 65–85). Springer.

Chapter 3
Exploring Opportunities for Critical Mental Health Social Work in Direct Practice: The Politics of Naming and Responding to Distress

The previous chapter (Chap. 2) acknowledged conceptualisations of mental health social work vary. Given the disconnect between social work's espoused values of social justice and the dignity of persons, and the colonial, neoliberal, and biomedical underpinnings of mental health services, the previous chapter identified numerous tensions and contradictions arising from the contextual influences on social work practice. This present chapter shifts the focus of our analysis towards examining the details of direct mental health social work *practice*—exploring what happens when social workers engage with and navigate such tensions (Whitaker et al., 2024). Although an awareness of power imbalances in the mental health field is widely acknowledged, transforming this analysis of power into practical actions can be very challenging (Brown, 2021). Consequently, mental health social work runs the risk of drifting towards clinical, prescriptive, and depoliticised practices, which offer certainty (Morley & Macfarlane, 2010), as we discussed in Chaps. 1 and 2. We seek to address the gap between an analysis of power and the minutiae of practice, by exploring how a power analysis has been relevant in our direct practice. In this way, we critically explore the role and contributions of mental health social work.

Our discussion aims to go beyond prescriptive and technocratic approaches to generic social work 'skills'; instead, we explore the possibilities that may open up when social workers are attuned to power arrangements and contexts. In doing this, it is not our intention to offer a reductionist or 'neat' version of social work direct practice in the mental health field. The practice examples are subjective and context-dependent and are not offered as ideal examples or universal approaches of the 'how-to' of social work practice within biomedical contexts; rather, they illustrate how we have navigated the challenges of biomedical neoliberalism in the mental health field, with varying degrees of impact.

This chapter outlines a range of ways of thinking and working that are informed by our reflections on *the politics of naming and responding to distress* when working with individuals. Chap. 4 continues the discussion by exploring the social work

L. Whitaker et al., *Social Work in the Mental Health Field*, SpringerBriefs in Social Work, https://doi.org/10.1007/978-3-032-08306-7_3

role in *navigating oppressive practices* within mental health service provision. However, to be responsive to the person and their circumstances, social work practice often involves several responses at any one time. We offer a range of practice possibilities which, at times, may seem somewhat messy. This reflects the complicated realities of navigating paradoxes and tensions when working within the mental health system (see Chap. 2), while also pointing towards opportunities for creativity and resistance when working within systems that are not aligned with social justice principles (Kelly & Chapman, 2015).

Responding to Distress

In identifying the violence (interpersonal, structural, and institutional) and responding to the distress that people are experiencing, this first section discusses how safety is not possible unless we attend to multiple dimensions of power, including but not limited to power in our relationships and in the physical spaces of mental health services, finding opportunities to challenge coercive practices, and to work towards an approach focused on partnership and solidarity, in contrast to a 'power over' or 'doing for' paradigm (Cameron & McGowan, 2013).

Attending to Power in Relationships

We discussed the importance of attending to power in the relationships and interactions that occur during the many 'generic' and taken-for-granted service provision processes. Before we have even met with a person, power is apparent in referral processes which often construct people in problematic and pathologising ways (Reid, 2023; Reid & Tseris, in press). It is difficult for people to articulate their concerns when they are unaware of the referral in the first instance and/or what has been included in the referral information. These potentially deficit-focused referral processes then influence the initial meeting with the person. For example, we discussed the importance of acknowledging that young people are not choosing to attend but are often 'sent' to a mental health service by an adult in their lives. Margaret explained:

> For young people it is often the very first time that they've stepped into a therapy space. So, they're already coming from a position of unknowing. They haven't chosen necessarily to be there. There's already lots of power in the room in terms of their parents' or caregivers' presence. [Therefore, my approach] in that first session, is to have very minimal problem talk.

We identified a major aspect of working in solidarity with a person is not assuming what the 'problem' is or what might be needed, to instead remain curious about what is important for the person. This is easier said than done, as we can default to assuming what the issue is and, therefore, what the most appropriate 'solution' should be. We explored how critical reflection can support us to maintain curiosity and humility (Fook, 2018), and to lean into discomfort and not knowing, in order to work towards embodying social justice principles in practice.

Consequently, we discussed strategies we have used, including how we take time to understand if the person actually wants to engage with the service, and what their hopes might be in accessing the service. To explore this with the person, Margaret explained how she asks the following questions: '*What are we going be doing together? What's going be helpful? What do you want to be different in your life?*' If the person identifies they want to engage, it is about then exploring *how* they want to work together, to avoid assumptions about what matters for them. For example, Scarlett reflected on working with a 12-year-old girl who had experienced multiple investigations through child protection services, which meant she was permanently removed from her family. She explained how:

> Questions represented a kind of interrogation, a power-over experience. Questions of any kind were really triggering for her. It was a real negotiation. I asked her how we were going to work together. She replied that I could take her to the local café, and I was not permitted to ask any questions and instead we would play a word game. And I said, 'Okay, then the next week you come to my office, and I get to ask four questions'. She was very good at reminding me when my question quota was up, so I had to make my questions really count. It was 12 months of not expecting anything more, because professional relationships were not safe for her. I think we're doing people a disservice to expect them to trust us, particularly children who have had their trust abused by adults, as we need to earn that trust.

This example illustrates how developing relationships can involve creativity and an openness to uncertainty and resisting the idea of being the 'expert'.

Initial points of connection were highlighted as key moments where thoughtful, and power astute ways of working were needed in order to develop a sense of safety for the person. Frankie explained the initial steps involved:

> Slowing that process down by exploring how somebody might arrive to wherever it is that you're working, how they might get there, how you might support them. I might take photos of the outside of the building or wherever we are and send those over. So being as invitational as possible. Let's talk about what the process of actually meeting each other is going to look like. Coming from trauma-informed practice means offering people as much choice and autonomy as possible, to build and be in relationship with somebody.

We also discussed how developing safety requires consistency and transparency, for example, '*showing up when I say I'm going to show up and following through on things I've promised*' (Scarlett).

Attending to Power in Physical Spaces

Bringing a power analysis also involved paying attention to the physical space in which we meet with people. Clinical spaces for some people can replicate the dynamics of previous experiences of violence or may not work for a variety of reasons.

Margaret spoke about the importance of introducing people to the building for those new to the space. She described how:

> This involves introducing the spaces and where they might be, and talking about who else is in the building, and where things are. Trying to give people as much information as possible, about where they are and where they're situated, because that's part of power. I think it's a way of trying to reduce the clinicians holding of knowledge and, therefore, holding power.

We can often lack imagination about alternative approaches and paradigms, and options beyond the confines of the organisational building can also be viewed as 'less professional' or 'more risky'. However, there are possibilities. Alyssa spoke about how *'it's always good to do outreach and meet people where they are at'*. Scarlett also shared a story of a 9-year-old girl she was working with. She described how:

> Some of our best chats happened when we decided to scooter at a local park. Some of our best thoughts were developed in motion. That was how we connected.

Being power astute included taking the time to consider the physical aspect of our work and what could be harmful about mainstream and taken-for-granted 'clinical' assumptions and practices, and considering other possibilities.

Exposing the Politics of Experience in the Mental Health System

In exposing the politics of experience in the mental health system, this next section explores how we have attempted to make visible socio-political contexts, elevate lived experience knowledges, exercise epistemic humility, recognise White privilege, and resist individualising approaches.

Making Visible Socio-Political Contexts and Elevating Lived Experience Knowledges

Within the biomedical model, clinical and evidence-based knowledge is prioritised over other possible framings of experiences, including socio-political, spiritual, cultural, and lived experience knowledges (as discussed in Chap. 2). This leads to the psychologisation of lived experiences (Rose, 2008). Because this hierarchy of knowledge subjugates experiential expertise, we discussed examples of practice where we have intentionally and thoughtfully tried to create space for, centring, and elevating first-person knowledges. This was seen as important because as Margaret explained:

> When people come to mental health services, their story is very much, 'there's something wrong with me', particularly with all the social media enticing them to find pathologising explanations.

We discussed the importance of being reflective about how we position ourselves in these interactions, recognising our own power as mental health professionals, working within a system that can disenfranchise people. We recognised how epistemic injustice occurs *'when there are certain kinds of knowledge that are respected more'* (Beatrice). Beatrice explains how this is *'an injustice, because the person's direct experience is invalidated'*. Fricker (2007) defines epistemic injustice as what 'occurs when prejudice causes a hearer to give a deflated level of credibility to a speaker's word' (p.1). This injustice is often shaped by structural prejudices, where the knowledges of groups with less power are silenced.

In contrast, epistemic justice is supported when a person is recognised for their lived experience and positioned as a legitimate 'knower' within the interaction (Johnstone, 2021). Epistemic practices can involve the person 'conveying knowledge to others by telling them and making sense of [their] own social experiences' (Fricker, 2007, p.1). It has, however, been noted that workers often engage with lived experience in ways that 'interpret' it, to try to fit it into existing professional understandings (Daya, 2020). We spoke about examples of when we have sought to challenge taken-for-granted assumptions made about people's lived experiences via clinical lens. We, therefore, discussed the importance of engaging with and learning from critical mental health and Mad Studies scholarship, which has offered more expansive, generative, and subversive paradigms of 'mental health', moving beyond the limitations of the professional project (Manchester, 2015; Sinclair et al., 2023).

We also explored how epistemic justice involves a lot more than listening to lived experience. Significant epistemic injustices have already occurred when someone has been labelled with or diagnosed with a mental disorder (Poole et al., 2012; Sweeney et al., 2019). Frankie described how social workers can begin by being curious, asking questions of inquiry, and listening carefully to the *'actual words used to describe their situation* and to explore *what they meant by those words'*. Scarlett described this as *'butterfly net listening, where you listen so closely to the words the person is using and if there is a key phrase you can scoop up carefully, like you're catching a butterfly'*. Instead of resorting to paraphrasing, Scarlett explained how using these key phrases and words can be valuable in elevating lived expertise in further collaborative conversations (White, 2012).

Our discussions revealed the ways in which we have tried to create space for the person to give voice to their lived experiences, and to make visible the wider contexts of their lives (Parker, 2018). As Frankie described, *'you're bringing the macro into the conversation'*. We discussed ways we have worked with individuals to collaboratively name the person's politics of experience, including gendered, racialised, and economic oppressions. This has led to unpacking various aspects of people's lives (Brown, 2020) in a way that has created more space for a socio-political conceptualisation of their lived experience (Kahn & Monk, 2017, p. 11).

These ways of talking about people's politics of experiences involved first and foremost, '*offering an invitation to explore the politics of experience and the macro with people*' (Frankie). We underscored the importance of invitational, gentle, and consensual approaches in these conversations. We recognised that consent is an essential aspect of ethical practice within a mental health system that is underpinned by formal and informal layers of coercion (Pelto-Piri et al., 2019). Sarah noted that we need to be careful about the power dynamics at play, even within conversations about social justice. This work is not about being the 'expert' or applying pressure to talk about violence or injustice:

> It is looking at the bigger picture, but it's also not about forcing it and understanding, especially with young people, there are issues around safety, both physical and emotional safety, when there is ongoing violence in their lives. We need to be careful about not applying pressure and to take the lead of young people in these conversations (Sarah).

We also explored how by moving away from positioning the person as 'the problem' we can open up possibilities for an alternative story of survival to become visible, rather than notions of 'individual pathology'. As Margaret explained:

> Being able to invite a different story by helping people make sense of their experiences and getting them to think about whether there is an alternative story. Those conversations around, 'you've lived in six different houses this year because your placements kept breaking down, no wonder it's been really hard to get to school. You've really been trying to survive and get to know all these new places. It makes sense that that's been really hard'.

In a number of instances, this involved drawing on the principles of narrative therapy, whereby the person is separated from the problem (White, 2007). In talking in these ways with the person, we are exploring events that do not fit with the 'dominant story' (often relating to diagnosis and deficits), to make visible an alternative story which reflects the person's preferred identity (White, 1995). As Sarah noted:

> By understanding the oppression people may be experiencing, the hope is to move away from 'the person is the problem' to look at the bigger picture.

We acknowledged how challenging it can be to separate the person from the problem and make visible the person's alternative story, when oppressive social structures in the person's life continue to perpetuate their distress (Reynolds, 2012). This includes the challenge of looking at and addressing this bigger picture in the context of the ongoing psychiatrisation of their experiences, within their broader experience of accessing mental health services (Beeker et al., 2020). To be able to explore potential alternative narratives about the person, we discussed opportunities to explore the person's experience of the mental health system and the power relations at work (Brown, 2024). As Barbie noted:

> I'm thinking I would talk with people about the macro and about how they've ended up here. I'm just thinking about public mental health particularly if they're on an involuntary

> treatment order of some kind… It's important to really position the system with their experiences and the way in which the system operates and what alternative narratives might have been and could be.

Margaret explained how she conceptualises this social justice approach as bringing a *political lens* in our conversations with the people we work with. She shared an example of practice with a young person:

> It feels like unpacking what people's experiences have been. I'm thinking about a young person who had recently been in hospital. It had been a really traumatic first presentation to mental health services. She was only 18 and she had never been in an adult mental health ward. I think bringing a political lens is about really unpacking what that experience was like for her.

This example demonstrates a commitment to acknowledging and attending to the significant injustices that can occur when people are on the receiving end of coercive mental health interventions. These practices involve inviting people to share stories, to make sense of their politics of experience, and explicitly unpack the power relations operating in their lives (Brown, 2021), rather than expecting people to accommodate to oppressive social conditions (Parker, 2018).

We recognised that bringing a power analysis to practice involved having conversations with people in ways that invited them to put words to the oppressive social structures they may be experiencing such as racism, sexism, ablism, and homophobia. As Barbie explained:

> So really making the implicit power relations explicit. For example, when working with young women, talking about the ways in which they've been oppressed as women. These conversations are not psychoeducation, it's really a political education. It is making visible the stuff that people know about and helping them create language around what people's individual experiences are. It's the sharing of knowledge.

We reflected on how we invite people to share lived experiences to identify and explore the operations of enduring power relations to support knowledge development (Reid & Alford, 2023); asking questions in ways that invite the person to make sense of their everyday experiences, to create distance from their immediate experiences of the bigger picture, and to scaffold their own understandings of the politics of their experiences to identify what matters to them the most (Reid, 2020). By unpacking these experiences of oppression, we identified how these conversations could provide space for peoples' survival skills to be acknowledged and explore their first-hand knowledges about systems that are positioned as benevolent, but may have been harmful (Kelly & Chapman, 2015).

The importance of elevating lived expertise in navigating coercive welfare and legal systems was underscored. As Frankie noted:

> People are very acutely aware, often, that they are in a political context. They're usually not using the same words that we are, but people have the skills and knowledges about our systems, which is usually far more in depth because they're living within this context. We might be using different language, but I think that's a part of the art of the conversation is to explore a person's skills and knowledges about the systems that they're in.

This is pertinent, as social workers are often positioned as holding expertise in systems navigation, and we may not adequately acknowledge the depth of skills and survival strategies emerging from direct experiences of systems. In addition to exploring system knowledges, we discussed how we can work with people to make visible their resistance and their skills in navigating the mental health system, while also prioritising advocacy as a key responsibility for social workers. Margaret offered an example of how she did this with a young woman who was admitted to an adult ward. She explained:

> After unpacking the young woman's experience of being in an adult ward, we explored, 'How did you navigate that? What got you through? What were the things that helped in that environment to be able to keep you connected to your previous self or identity?' And then thinking about what kind of knowledge can she impart from her experience. For example, she's been very clear about what was not helpful in her previous hospital presentation. So, helping her to put that in a document so that if she goes to hospital in the future, she's got that sense of a bit more power and control to be clear around what's helpful.

These examples demonstrate how social workers can play a role in creating space for lived experience knowledges with the aim to unpack oppression and to co-produce understandings, rather than adopting a 'power-over' approach to advocacy, while also demonstrating the harms of coercive practices within the systems in which social work is enacted and the need for social workers to actively challenge such practices (see Chap. 4).

In making visible peoples' survival skills and knowledges, we are also leaning into the complexity of peoples' lives and recognising there are times of not-knowing. For example, Sarah discussed:

> We are not just replicating this kind of cause-and-effect type of thinking within a social approach, where we can unintentionally enact a prescriptive or 'diagnostic' approach, even when talking about issues of social justice. Instead, we are somehow leaning into the complexity of peoples' lives and not knowing. We might make some links between social contexts and distress, but they're also tentative and they don't necessarily become a new simplistic story in a person's life.

Sarah's example reminds us to reconsider a position of certainty in our social work practice and how we aspire to make space for multiple perspectives and diverse forms of meaning-making in our practice (Bhattacharya, 2016).

We also recognised that centring and elevating lived experiences within a therapeutic context is only the start of critical mental health practice, as therapy alone cannot address or overcome structural inequities. We, therefore, questioned any single approach—even if it has 'progressive' potential, such as narrative therapy—to avoid positioning it as a panacea for addressing the impacts of socio-political oppression in people's lives. While we fostered the conditions for people to give voice and make sense of their experiences, we were mindful to avoid therapising peoples' experiences of social injustice and oppression (Ecclestone & Brunila, 2015). Timor-Shlevin (2023) explains the limitations of 'isolated emotional support' which value the 'service users' voices' … but at the same time 'overlooks service users' material needs' (p.32). We recognised this as a priority, because peoples' lives are inherently entangled with their socio-cultural and material environments. For example, if someone is living in poverty and facing homelessness, we discussed the need to work holistically and practically with the person. Consequently, while we were inviting people to give voice to the politics of their experiences, we also recognised we have a key responsibility to not only 'talk' about the social structures that perpetuate their distress but also find ways to practically address them.

Exercising Epistemic Humility and Recognising White Privilege

Our discussions identified the relevance of exercising epistemic humility when centring and elevating people's politics of experience, including analysing the White privilege that we may bring into the interaction, and the importance of recognising social work's active participation in an array of institutional racist policies, such as the Stolen Generations (Walter et al., 2011). Frankie reminded us that '*social work often produces harm through failing to notice Whiteness in the room*'. When Whiteness is not acknowledged, certain perspectives can become dominant, while marginalising other forms of meaning-making. Barbie reflected:

> If we're truly practicing from our anti-oppressive, person-centred approach and trauma-informed position, we work with what's in the room. So, we will be taking the lead from the person that we're working with. We need to understand how they're making meaning of what's happening.

We discussed the applicability of ongoing critical reflection to make ourselves accountable in the work, as we agreed that we cannot simply claim that we are working in a 'decolonising' or 'culturally safe' manner (Tujague & Ryan, 2021). Indeed, even the notion of 'cultural competence' can invite complacency and superficial engagement with learning a set of skills rather than engaging with more important (and sometimes uncomfortable) questions about power, professionalism, and privilege (Yassine & Tseris, 2022). To be able to understand how people are making meaning from their cultural standpoint, we first recognised our own social positioning (Sue et al., 2007). Depending on our own social positioning we may be afforded 'unearned privileges attached to whiteness' (Yassine & Tseris, 2022, p. 197). For example, Scarlett reflected on walking into meetings about a First Nation young people she was working with and described how '*I had to be constantly aware of this White Western standpoint that I was bringing into the room and the weight of colonial history*'. To add to this, Barbie also noted that:

> As a person born into the colonial position in Australia, I sometimes feel uncomfortable about acknowledging that oppression when working with First Nations folk. I want to raise this because I think that's really important for emerging social workers to recognise discomfort and go with it anyway. Because if it's on the table then we can talk about the construction of mental health from an imperialist colonial, male, Western lens, which is just the antithesis of so many people's understandings of emotional health and well-being.

In this way, Barbie described how moving towards cultural safety involves an ongoing critical examination of ourselves, our professional positioning and the institutional structures in which we work, which are informed by racist assumptions. Lorde (1997) defines racism as 'the belief in the inherent superiority of one race over all others and thereby the right to dominance' (p. 496). Our discussions revealed the need to remain vigilant to any professional assumptions which may subjugate First Nation knowledges and ways of being.

Unlike White privilege, trust needs to be earned. To exercise humility and to embody social justice in this relational work, we '*can only go at the pace of trust, which really contrasts with the KPI's and the very outcomes-focused approach*' (Frankie). Scarlett also spoke about the importance of considering cultural safety in our meeting places.

> I met young people in community rather than expecting people to come to the clinic, to fit into this White Western model. I met people where they felt the most comfortable and that was often outdoors. We would shoot hoops, and I got a lot of advice on how to improve my netball shooting because clearly, I had some netball issues that needed to be addressed!

To listen and learn from Indigenous knowledges, we reflected on how First Nations perspectives on social and emotional wellbeing are shaped by a lens of collectivism, and grounded in traditions, kinship, community connection, and Country rather than individual conceptions (Gone, 2021; Mehl-Madrona & Mainguy, 2021). Alyssa explained how she is '*really influenced by the social and emotional well-being framework*' (Dudgeon et al., 2017). She described the intersecting seven domains including connection to body, connection to mind and emotions, connection to family and kinship, connection to community, connection to culture, connection to Country, and connection to spirituality and ancestors (Dudgeon et al., 2017). Alyssa reflected on how social and emotional wellbeing is possible when there is connection across all the domains and how this differs substantially from Western models of mental health. Alyssa said she takes time to understand what connection means, '*because every community is different*' and there is no one-size-fits-all approach that can be applied.

Our reflections demonstrated that social work could play a role in meeting the person alongside key people such as Aunts and Uncles, in their everyday lives and their communities, and indeed, could draw on advocacy skills and a critical systems approach to perhaps avoid contact with mainstream mental health services altogether. In contrast to a persistent focus on referring people to mental health services, we discussed how the social work role can involve supporting people to access the resources they might need, while remaining outside of the mental health system, as a referral could be a retraumatising and culturally inappropriate response (Miller et al., 2025). Community-based alternatives to 'clinical' mental health services are explored further in Chap. 5.

Resisting Individualising Approaches by Privileging Relational Worlds

Despite the dominant focus on working with individuals in mental health service provision, our discussions explored the value of considering the broader relational world of a person, including how healing can happen in the context of certain relationships and communities. This may or may not involve meeting or building relationships with the key people in a person's life. It could involve simply recognising what these key relationships mean to them and acknowledging the role they play in the person's life. These relationships may be current, past, or with people who have passed away. This relational approach was intentional, as we identified how there is a persistent minimisation of social networks and communities around a person within mainstream mental health practice. For example, Margaret describes how she invites key people in a young person's life to join the conversation, if this feels safe and meaningful for the young person:

> By having someone from the person's real world come into the room, I wonder, then, if the conversation can go from that room and back into the real world. I wonder if that makes it feel more real. When I'm first meeting young people, my starting activity is a strengths card activity where they'll choose something that represents them and then their family member does the same. It's been really lovely seeing young people get a sense of what others notice and appreciate about them. It surprises me how often the young people are surprised.

Involving significant people can challenge and disrupt an 'individual clinical work' focus. Importantly, in Margaret's example, it was not about gathering more data about 'the problem' but was about enabling the person to recognise their strengths and community, to explore how they have coped despite their circumstances. This practice, therefore, aimed to create space to explore resistances to injustice, and to challenge a deficit and pathologising narrative about the person. Scarlett explains how she gave young women who had experienced sexual assault the option to invite a close friend (where this was something that they wanted) to join some conversations. She described how having a best friend present enabled:

> the acknowledgement of the injustice that the young woman had experienced and bear witness to how the young woman was recovering. It made some of those survival skills more real for the young women. If we had spoken about how they've been coping with just myself and the young woman, it may have less impact. But having a young woman's best friend, say 'I've noticed you doing this and wow, it just blows me away, how you've done this, despite what has happened'. The survival skills became more real because it was acknowledged by significant people in their lives.

Scarlett reflected on how inviting key people to become involved in collaborative conversations was helpful for a number of reasons, particularly to guard against isolation and a clinical focus on an individual with 'the problem', in order to make visible the injustice, people's resistance and survival skills.

Our discussions also illustrated how we have explored with people how they have stayed connected during times of adversity. For instance, Frankie described her work with incarcerated women:

> The ways that women will create community, even in the most difficult situation, in terms of being isolated and individualised. You know, you've been taken into this prison system. You've been taken away from your community, your family, your children, your work, your home, everything has been taken from you. And still women will find ways to create community… even in isolating situations. I think acknowledging that is really important because sometimes we can go in with this perspective that it's not happening, but people will always find ways.

This example is reflective of other research on experiences in involuntary mental health treatment settings, where people find ways to build community, even within contexts of extreme isolation and a denial of rights (Tseris et al., 2024). Frankie's example demonstrates recognising resistance involves identifying the nuanced ways in which people actively respond to oppression (Burstow, 1992; Wade, 1997), including understanding the community-building that is already happening without social work involvement.

Working relationally also involved considering non-human connections that support peoples' wellbeing. We explored how it was not just human relationships we have tried to privilege in our work with individuals. For example, Scarlett noted:

> In my work with children in care we would talk about pets. They had some really key relationships with animals in their lives. Even if they were not with that animal anymore, some of our chats were what these relationships meant for them. Often children described how the family dog would greet them with unconditional positive regard irrespective of what trouble they had experienced in their day.

While many of our examples relate to privileging people's relational worlds with humans and animals, we also discussed the importance of exploring people's connection to culture and Country (Dudgeon et al., 2021). Alyssa described a First Nations social work perspective, including how she works with Aboriginal people by unpacking:

> What connection to Country and community and culture means for that person and how that connection is leveraged to keep them well. I will ask someone 'Where you from? Who's your Country? Who's your mob? Have you ever been back on Country? What does connecting to Country look like to you?' It's about facilitating a conversation, a brainstorming session about those domains.

Alyssa further explained how:

> Every Aboriginal person I've seen has experienced and continues to experience some level of psychosocial distress that is completely and utterly out of their control and so the only way you can address that, is through building up their protective factors like connection to culture and Country.

We recognised how '*people can feel really isolated—they may have received the message that the distress is about them individually and that they are an individual failure*' (Beatrice). While we explored how to privilege existing relationships, we also discussed opportunities to consider linking people beyond their immediate and current network. Beatrice explained there is:

> The need for people to recognise their place in the larger context. It's about linking people up. For me it's about moving away from the individual into the collective. It's a way of moving people towards groupwork with people who have had similar experiences because it's actually not about individuals, it's about the way in which society is set up.

While community work will be explored further in Chap. 5, we highlighted the ways that social workers can consider opportunities to connect people across shared experiences of resisting injustice, even when working individually in 'clinical' settings. Frankie explained that in order to do this, we actually '*need the time to link and connect and build relationships within the community*'. In this way, we can become more attuned to a collective rather than clinical response to injustice, thus attending to socio-political contexts, and challenging the persistent focus within mainstream mental health services on fixing individual 'symptoms'.

Conclusion

Navigating the complex terrain of the mental health field to engage with individuals in a way that enacts social justice is challenging, to say the least. Moving beyond merely identifying this challenge, this chapter has provided a window into how social work practice engages with the many contradictions involved in enacting change within oppressive systems. In the hierarchy of knowledges within multidisciplinary teams, socio-political understandings and lived experience knowledges are marginalised (Sweeney et al., 2019). A key focus of the chapter was on what it takes to work towards the conditions that support epistemic justice, so that people's voices and knowledges about the politics of experiences can be heard and made more visible. The White, Western paradigm in the mental health system is pervasive. While there has been an intention to explore the dynamics involved in working with individuals in this chapter, individuals are inherently interconnected within relationships, systems, and Country. Consequently, our analysis has revealed the relevance of privileging socio-political and relational worlds when working with individuals, in order to move past a relentless focus on individual or clinical recovery (Price-Robertson et al., 2017), towards a more expansive set of possibilities for understanding and responding to distress.

References

Beeker, T., Witeska-Młynarczyk, A., te Meerman, S., & Mills, C. (2020). Psychiatrization of, with and by children: Drawing a complex picture. *Global Studies of Childhood, 10*(1), 12–25.

Bhattacharya, A. (2016). The many ways of knowing: Embracing multiplicity in narrative research. *Qualitative Social Work, 15*(5–6), 705–714.

Brown, C. (2020). Critical clinical social work: Theoretical and practical considerations. In C. Brown & J. McDonald (Eds.), *Critical clinical social work: Counterstorying for social justice* (pp. 16–58). Canadian Scholars' Press.

Brown, C. (2021). Critical clinical social work and the neoliberal constraints on social justice in mental health. *Research on Social Work Practice, 31*(6), 644–652.

Brown, C. (2024). Reframing trauma through social justice resisting the politics of mainstream trauma discourse. Taylor & Francis Group.

Burstow, B. (1992). *Radical feminist therapy*. Sage.

Cameron, D., & McGowan, P. (2013). The mental health social worker as a transitional participant: actively listening to 'voices' and getting into the recovery position. *Journal of Social Work Practice, 27*(1), 21–32.

Daya, I., Hamilton, B., & Roper, C. (2020). Authentic engagement: A conceptual model for welcoming diverse and challenging consumer and survivor views in mental health research, policy, and practice. *International Journal of Mental Health Nursing, 29*(2), 299–311. https://doi.org/10.1111/inm.12653

Dudgeon, P., Bray, A., D'costa, B., & Walker, R. (2017). Decolonising psychology: Validating social and emotional wellbeing. *Australian Psychologist, 52*(4), 316–325.

Dudgeon, P., Blustein, S., Bray, A., Calma, T., McPhee, R & Ring, I. (2021). *Connection between family, kinship and social and emotional wellbeing.* Indigenous mental health and suicide prevention clearinghouse. Cat. no. IMH 4. Australian Institute of Health and Welfare.

Ecclestone, K., & Brunila, K. (2015). Governing emotionally vulnerable subjects and 'therapisation'of social justice. *Pedagogy, Culture & Society, 23*(4), 485–506.

Fook, J. (2018). *Social work: A critical approach to practice*. Sage.

Fricker, M. (2007). *Epistemic injustice: Power and the ethics of knowing*. Oxford University Press.

Gone, J. P. (2021). The (post)colonial predicament in community mental health services for American Indians: Explorations in alter-native psy-ence. *American Psychologist, 76*(9), 1514–1525.

Johnstone, M. (2021). Centering social justice in mental health practice: Epistemic justice and social work practice. *Research on Social Work Practice, 31*(6), 634–643.

Kahn, S., & Monk, G. (2017). Narrative supervision as a social justice practice. *Journal of Systemic Therapies, 36*(1), 7–25.

Kelly, C., & Chapman, C. (2015). Adversarial allies: Care, harm, and resistance in the helping professions. *Journal of Progressive Human Services, 26*(1), 46–66.

Lorde, A. (1997). Age, race, class, and sex: Women redefining difference. *Cultural Politics, 11*, 374–380.

Manchester, R. (2015). Towards critical mental health social work: Learning from critical psychiatry and psychiatry survivors. *Critical and Radical Social Work, 3*(1), 149–154.

Mehl-Madrona, L., & Mainguy, B. (2021). Indigenous mental health in remote communities. In T. A. Carey & J. Gullifer (Eds.), *Handbook of rural, remote, and very remote mental health* (pp. 67–92). Springer Nature.

Miller, K., Morda, R., & Sonn, C. C. (2025). Tokenistic or transformative? An exploration of culturally safe care in Australian mental health nursing. *International Journal of Mental Health, 54*(1), 4–21.

Morley, C., & Macfarlane, S. (2010). Repositioning social work in mental health: Challenges and opportunities for critical practice. *Critical Social Work, 11*(2), 46–59.

Parker, I. (2018). Marxist theory and psychotherapy. In B. M. Z. Cohen (Ed.), *Routledge international handbook of critical mental health* (pp. 244–250). Routledge.

Pelto-Piri, V., Kjellin, L., Hyléen, U., Valenti, E., & Priebe, S. (2019). Different forms of informal coercion in psychiatry: a qualitative study. *BMC Research Notes, 12*, 1–4.

Poole, J. M., Jivraj, T., Arslanian, A., Bellows, K., Chiasson, S., Hakimy, H., et al. (2012). Sanism, 'mental health', and social work/education: A review and call to action. *Intersectionalities: A Global Journal of Social Work Analysis Research, Polity, and Practice, 1*, 20–36.

Price-Robertson, R., Obradovic, A., & Morgan, B. (2017). Relational recovery: beyond individualism in the recovery approach. *Advances in Mental Health, 15*(2), 108–120.

Sinclair, A., Mahboub, L., Gillieatt, S., & Fernandes, C. (2023). 'You just treat me like a human being': Using lived experience to (re) imagine boundary practices in mental health settings. *The British Journal of Social Work, 53*(3), 1408–1425.

Tujague, N., & Ryan, K. (2021). Ticking the box of 'cultural safety' is not enough: Why trauma-informed practice is critical to indigenous healing. *Rural and Remote Health, 21*.

Reid, K. (2020). Reaching higher ground: The importance of Lev Vygotsky's therapeutic legacy for social work. In Morley, C., Ablett, P., Noble, C. & Cowden, S. (Eds.), *The Routledge handbook of critical pedagogies for social work* (pp. 58–70). Routledge.

Reid, K. (2023). Who has naming rights? The framing of children's mental health issues in discursive therapy with their caregivers. *Child & Family Social Work, 29*(1), 48–57.

Reid, K., & Tseris, E. (in press). Precarious epistemic justice: Navigating the politics of the therapy room with children and their caregivers. *Feminism and Psychology.*

Reid, K., & Alford, J. (2023). Empowerment or holding the child responsible? An Australian recovery-oriented mental health policy analysis. *British Journal of Social Work, 53*(5), 2860–2877.

Rose, N. (2008). Psychology as a social science. *Subjectivity, 25*, 446–462.

Reynolds, V. (2012). Bridging the worlds of therapy and activism: Intersections, tensions and affinities. *International Journal of Narrative Therapy & Community Work, 4*, 57–61.

Sweeney, A., Perôt, C., Callard, F., Adenden, V., Mantovani, N., & Goldsmith, L. (2019). Out of the silence: towards grassroots and trauma-informed support for people who have experienced sexual violence and abuse. *Epidemiology and Psychiatric Sciences, 28*(6), 598–602.

Sue, D. W., Capodilupo, C. M., Torino, G. C., Bucceri, J. M., Holder, A. M. B., Nadal, K. L., & Esquilin, M. (2007). Racial microaggressions in everyday life: Implications for clinical practice. *The American Psychologist, 62*(4), 271–286.

Timor-Shlevin, S. (2023). Conceptualizing critical practice in social work: An integration of recognition and redistribution. *European Journal of Social Work, 26*(1), 28–40.

Tseris, E., Franks, S., & Hart, E. B. (2024). Psychiatric oppression in women's lives: Creative resistance and collective dissent (1st ed.). Springer International Publishing. https://doi.org/10.1007/978-3-031-65068-0

Wade, A. (1997). Small acts of living: Everyday resistance to violence and other forms of oppression. *Contemporary Family Therapy, 19*, 23–39.

Walter, M., Taylor, S., & Habibis, D. (2011). How white is social work in Australia? *Australian Social Work, 64*(1), 6–19.

Whitaker, L., Smith, F., Velander, F., Petrakis, M., Deacon, E., Simboli, T., et al. (2024). Mental health social work practice: navigating tensions. *The British Journal of Social Work, 54*(6), 2565–2582.

White, M. (1995). *Re-authoring lives: interviews and essays*. Dulwich Centre.

White, M. (2007). *Maps of narrative practice* (1st ed.). W.W. Norton & Co..

White, M. (2012). Scaffolding a therapeutic conversation. In T. Malinen, S. Cooper, & F. Thomas (Eds.), *Masters of narrative and collaborative therapies: The voices of Andersen, Anderson, and White* (pp. 121–170). Routledge.

Yassine, L., & Tseris, E. (2022). From rhetoric to action: confronting whiteness in social work and transforming practices. *Critical and Radical Social Work, 10*(2), 192–208.

Chapter 4
Exploring Opportunities for Critical Mental Health Social Work in Direct Practice: Navigating Oppressive Practices

While mental health practice alleviates distress in some cases, it is also oppressive in the lives of many people (Tseris et al., 2024). The pervasive use of coercion in mental health service provision sits at odds with social work values of social justice (Maylea, 2017). Taken-for-granted and overused buzzwords, including 'trauma-informed', 'strengths-based', and 'recovery-oriented' discourses can conceal the ongoing epistemic injustice and violence occurring within the mental health system (Tseris, 2019; Reid et al., 2024; Reid & Alford, 2023; Reid et al., in press). This chapter extends on Chap. 3, by unpacking ethical challenges that social workers face in the mental health field and exploring social work responses to oppressive practices. It goes beyond working with individuals, to explore critical social work practices in organisations, within multidisciplinary teams, and within wider systems. This chapter explores ways to re-conceptualise risk, to engage in advocacy and anti-oppressive documentation, to build strategic multidisciplinary relationships, and to foster creativity and joy.

These illustrations of practice, depicting how individual social workers have navigated complex ethical challenges, do not offer simple solutions or clear-cut answers as to how social work can disrupt and subvert oppression in the mental health field. The examples are diverse, with some being small and everyday acts of resistance, while other examples are more explicitly attempting to recognise and address oppressive practices on a more systemic level. Some of the examples raise questions about how social workers may be co-opted into supporting biomedical and neoliberal paradigms, even in their attempt to challenge taken-for-granted assumptions within their organisational contexts. In sharing our discussions and examples of practice, we hope to evoke further critical reflection of social work's positioning as a profession within the mental health field, while also inspiring further opportunities for both small and larger acts of resistance. As we discuss further in Chap. 6, the research process itself was a generative process in opening possibilities to 'think otherwise' about mental health (Fullagar, 2018), offering an important

L. Whitaker et al., *Social Work in the Mental Health Field*, SpringerBriefs in Social Work, https://doi.org/10.1007/978-3-032-08306-7_4

opportunity for collective, creative conversations, accountability and critical reflection on the politics and ethics of direct practice in mental health social work.

Moving Beyond the Buzzwords: Extending Recovery, Strengths-Based, and Trauma-Informed Approaches

Our discussions highlighted how various buzzwords such as 'strengths-based', 'person-centred', 'recovery-oriented', and 'trauma-informed' are frequently spoken about in the mental health field but have become superficially enacted. For example, Cassidy noted that *'person-centred care is social work 101, but it's actually incredibly complex to find ways to do this; in some systems this can be quite compromising'*. Theoretical conceptualisations of these approaches are well-aligned with social work values, as they speak to a nuanced appreciation of the influences of lived experience and social contexts. However, social work's positioning in the mental health system can render practitioners complicit in offering an individualised and superficial application of these approaches. This can be of further concern as Scarlett explained:

> It's almost like there is a single story that social work is inherently empowering and person-centred. This professional narrative whitewashes the many contradictions of social work practice in the mental health field.

We recognised the need to unpack key contradictions when working in biomedically dominated settings, if we are to resist superficial ways of enacting recovery and trauma-informed approaches. For instance, Barbie questioned the very concept of 'recovery' by asking *'what are people actually recovering from? There's recovery from oppression rather than distress, but I think the mental health system is set up around recovery from distress'*.

While we discussed the importance of recognising peoples' strengths, ways of coping and survival skills, we were aware of the hazard of a superficial rendition of strengths-based practice. Although strengths-based practice was initially articulated as a response to the dominance of a deficit-focused approach in the mental health field, it can easily be applied in ways that fail to address oppressive social structures (Askew et al., 2020; Gray, 2011). We recognised that using strengths-based language is insufficient in enacting social justice. The ongoing power imbalances are in operation from the beginning of our interactions with people, at the point of referral onwards (as discussed in Chap. 3). Askew et al. (2020, p.104) argue that 'a strengths-based approach required a relinquishment of the power imbalance implicit in the client/service provider relationships'. We discussed how we enact more power astute ways to stand in solidarity with people from the outset and recognise that strengths can include a broad array of actions in resisting intersecting oppressions.

Our discussions explored opportunities to go beyond the buzzwords to more meaningfully consider ethical practice, aligned with social justice principles. To navigate such contradictions, our discussions considered a range of subversive acts (Laing & Maylea, 2018) when working in biomedically dominated contexts to enact a power analysis in practice. Portelli and Eizadirad (2018) define subversive acts as any act with the intention to:

> stand up to injustice and inequitable practices as a means of rupturing the status quo… and harnessing hope for change and opening up of new possibilities. At the core of subversion is an understanding that everyday decisions and actions have consequences far beyond the surface level and… impact others in numerous ways (p. 54–55).

These acts of resistance may not be large in scope; rather, they may be covert or fragmented examples (Greenslade et al., 2015; Carey & Foster, 2011). For example, spending time including children's voice into a mental health 'formulation' can be a small yet significant way to push back on the privileging of 'expert' clinical knowledge which is the antithesis of espoused 'recovery' approaches. As Scarlett described:

> There are so many contradictions that we need speak about in terms of 'recovery' approaches. We are expected to assess, diagnose and formulate a treatment plan, which excludes the child or young person's voice. So, I'd spend quite a lot of time trying to get key quotes from the child regardless of their age, to try to incorporate their words into the assessment and the treatment plan. I have found children have firm and clear ideas from quite an early age as to what matters to them. In my previous service, we engaged children right from the start of the intake process by asking the 'miracle question' or 'magic wand' questions about what they hope to be different in their lives. It's such a simple question, but I think it's such an important one to ask.

Other examples of resistance involved how we engage with people in 'recovery planning'. Margaret noted the impacts of generic 'recovery planning' with children who have survived violence and abuse and identified how this process could actually invite them to experience failure. She explained:

> If they haven't experienced hope yet or had opportunities to really think about what a different life could be, then it becomes another thing of, 'Oh, now I can't even think of anything that I want to do'.

Here is an example of when a 'strengths-based' approach, which might be considered an inherently empowering paradigm, can be enacted as a harmful institutional practice. Organisational processes can place pressure on the social worker to undertake a 'recovery plan' in a certain timeframe, but Margaret articulated that working with children who are experiencing distress:

> really needs to be built on across time, whereby children are supported to develop a relationship where they are seen and heard… we can get more of an understanding of what their needs are and then their 'recovery plan' will become more meaningful.

Pushing back on unrealistic timeframes, to take the time to learn from the person to ensure their lived expertise informs these clinical processes such as 'assessment', 'treatment', and 'recovery planning' is a form of resistance. These examples illustrate how organisational expectations and practices can co-opt concepts—including 'recovery'—which have arisen from the survivor movement—and dilute the principles into rigid organisational procedures that actually cause harm (Logan &

Carter, 2022). To challenge this, we explored how we have sought to engage with questions about power in everyday practice, and to consider opportunities for 'intentionally small-scale practice behaviours of caring resistance' (Laing & Maylea, 2018, p.24).

Similar to recovery-oriented approaches, trauma-informed approaches in mental health are very well-regarded, yet further critical examination is needed to explore how these approaches are enacted within mental health organisations (Tseris, 2019). By superficially applying trauma-informed 'techniques', we can easily overlook the power relations at play when someone is accessing mental health services. We questioned how 'trauma-informed' organisations are, when people with experiences of violence are experiencing further violations within the process of accessing 'help'. For example, Beatrice noted in situations of involuntary treatment orders and admission:

> actually being in hospital at that moment or being detained against their will isn't going to help. That's going to be more frightening. And the person's going to want to go home because they feel like they're captured. They might be able to stay for some rest if they weren't there against their will.

It was repeatedly noted that significant violations can occur while trying to access support. In these instances, we identified strategies to acknowledge the injustice of what has occurred, first and foremost, and in collaboration with the person. For example, Scarlett described a situation when she was working with a boy who was assaulted by co-tenants in a new residential placement. She explained:

> I wanted to acknowledge what had happened because no one else really had. So, I said to him 'I'm really sorry that you weren't kept safe and the system has let you down'. Unless we can acknowledge this wrongdoing, how can people heal? Even though it was not my decision to change his placement, I wanted to make clear that 'every child has a right to feel safe and you were put in situation which was unsafe and I'm really sorry about this and it is not OK'.

This example clearly demonstrates the 'problem' does not reside within the individual and the importance in social work of refusing a neutral position in response to violence. In addition, the example warrants further exploration of the role of social work in responding to institutional violations. Beyond naming injustices, our role includes systemic forms of resistance, and advocacy and ultimately, refusing complicity in harmful systems (Scarlett's decision to leave this workplace is discussed in more detail in Chap. 5).

Our discussions illuminated how 'trauma-informed' approaches are increasingly imbued with assumptions which decontextualise the person's experiences of oppression (Brown, 2020, 2024; Tseris, 2019). Such psychological and individualised applications of trauma-informed approaches focus on the person's 'symptoms', with the aim to support them to better manage them (Johnstone & Lee, 2024). This leads to:

> a narrow focus on symptom assessment, treatment modalities, and neurobiological processes precludes a myriad of other possibilities for understanding gender-based violence and effectively responding to patriarchal contexts beyond medical and therapeutic contexts (Tseris, 2019, p. 108).

With this individualised treatment focus, the perspectives of people who have endured violence may be marginalised and silenced (Tseris, 2019), causing further epistemic injustice. Instead of exploring the person's understandings, as Scarlett stated, *'it becomes an expectation to learn therapeutic strategies (such as grounding techniques and mindfulness) to 'self-regulate', irrespective of what's occurring in your life'*. Rather than placing the responsibility of recovery onto the individual, we considered how social workers can explore ways to support epistemic justice by recognising the bigger picture of the person's life and the power relationships operating (Brown, 2021). Yet, within diagnostic systems, we reflected on *'how easy it is for people who are experiencing tactics of control and abuse to develop that story that they are powerless'* (Scarlett) and for their strategies of resistance to be either unnoticed, or even pathologised. We discussed how we seek to avoid pathologising narratives while making visible people's survival knowledge and skills in the context of violence. This was not an attempt to highlight people's resilience irrespective of the violence (Askew et al., 2020; Gray, 2011) but to expose the tactics of power at work. For example, Scarlett explains how this type of practice involves:

> Trying to highlight the initiatives and steps that the woman was taking to spot those power relationships occurring in her life, to explore how despite those oppressive forces, what she was managing to do or achieve, despite those awful ways of being treated.

In these discussions, we reflected on how meaningful trauma-informed approaches involve much more than therapeutic techniques, instead incorporating an intentionally relational approach, alongside an ethical commitment to reflecting on the multiple layers of power operating in people's lives, including 'denouncing atrocities and demanding justice' (Tseris, 2019, p. 110). In this way, trauma-informed approaches can involve asking questions of ourselves, including *'how I'm in relationship and solidarity with somebody'* (Frankie). This is not about a checklist approach, nor we can ever make the claim that we have fully enacted trauma-informed care, within imperfect and oppressive systems.

Reconceptualising Risk

When navigating the contradictions and paradoxes in mental health social work, we noted how interactions with risk-averse mental health organisations can contribute to, rather than alleviate distress. We acknowledged how many of us have worked in risk-adverse settings, describing how *'workers are doing what they need to do to cover themselves. And meanwhile, people are left with very little support or resources'* (Sarah). We discussed how this risk-oriented approach is often more about managing the risk for the organisation as opposed to holding the risk with a person who is experiencing distress. For instance, Beatrice questioned involuntary treatment saying: *'does this person really need this at the moment or is it just because we're worried with our own risk rather than their risk?'* This 'risk management' approach is often used to justify increased surveillance and coercion (Oaten,

2022). Sarah explained that the system responds to risk with either '*coercion or abandonment, set up as the only two options, as though nothing else is possible'*. This raises important questions regarding how social work can contribute to developing options and practices beyond such binary responses.

Our discussions revealed the need to question and review risk assessment practices. While there is pressure to engage in risk assessments to 'regulate the uncertain' (Oaten et al., 2022, p. 670), we explored times when we have tried to avoid coercive approaches to 'risk management'. Scarlett described a situation where the organisation had concerns about the safety of a young woman she was working with. There was a pattern where self-harm increased when she separated from her boyfriend. Scarlett explained her awareness of the broader context:

> Both her parents had been incarcerated and one of them had died in incarceration. So, there was significant trauma in her back story. Our psychiatrist, at the time, was very nervous about the risk on this particular day and felt that we should involve the police and the ambulance to just take her in. I thought to myself, we first and foremost could visit her... In reflection, if we involved the police, this would have been very triggering for her, given her parents' negative contact with the police and how it would have negatively impacted my relationship with her. So why would we take a heavy-handed approach when we're actually meant to be acting in a least restrictive way?

This example demonstrates how social workers may find themselves negotiating diverse and competing views on 'risk' across a multidisciplinary team. As Beatrice reflected:

> Once you have established relationships you can assess the situation from a perspective that is informed by your relationship. So, you were able to bring a range of factors to an assessment. To know it's not dangerous to go to the home, because you've assessed this situation, and you know this person.

While the priorities of the psychiatrist in the above example were centred on acting on a very narrow conceptualisation of 'risk', in this case, a social work lens made space for a broader understanding of context, power, and institutional violence. This allowed for a response that was relationally informed, including an understanding of the detrimental impacts of coercive practices and professionals making decisions and intervening on behalf of others (Davidson et al., 2016; Ross, 2020). At the same time, this example raises significant questions regarding the social work role within mental health services, and how mental health social workers can quite easily be co-opted into participation in risk-averse practices. When trying to minimise harm within biomedical settings, we may be expected to comply with paternalism and 'social control masquerading as care' (Manchester, 2015, p.152). Critical social work literature has noted social work's professional responsibility 'to provide support, when early intervention might prevent further deterioration and avert other harm to that person or those around them' (Maylea, 2017, p. 341). Crucially, this critique of risk aversion acknowledges that people experiencing distress have a right to access support and resources of their choosing and that such rights should not be used as a justification for involuntary treatment (Maylea, 2017).

Despite mental health services focusing on assessing 'risk' within individuals, other discussions illustrated examples of working within systems that are refusing to respond to structural risks, including violence and homelessness, whereby articulating 'risk' discourses could become useful by *'using the dominant paradigm defensively as an advocacy tool'* (Sarah). For example, Frankie explained:

> I am going to use the 'clinical' and policy language in a way that's going to best serve the person that I am supporting. It's using the language of policies and procedures of organisations to advocate towards increased accountability.

This demonstrates opportunities for social workers to use an organisation's resources and to elegantly navigate its discourses towards social justice, through 'concerted and sustained efforts' (Kelly & Chapman, 2015, p.63). However, this too is not without challenges and tensions. As Manchester, (2015) notes, when social workers use medical language in our work, this reinforces and perpetuates the legitimacy of the medical model.

Neoliberalism can construct the individual as if they are an 'island', separate from social support networks (Brown, 2021). Our discussions demonstrated how we have tried to re-conceptualise assumptions about 'risk' by considering people in the context of their support networks and wider communities. As Margaret noted *'the first step of least restrictive practice is, exploring who's already around, who's part of the person's community, who's part of those informal networks'*. Iris explained how she was able to question the use of involuntary treatment, by stating:

> It wasn't just the relationship I had with the person. I also had the awareness that this person was living in a community that really did support them and did know this person really well. They'd lived there all their lives. The community members knew when this person wasn't well and would let us know. So we didn't need to carry all of the risk. The community was actually carrying some of that risk.

Engaging with risk in a more relational way also involves having conversations with the person outside of a crisis to explore potential responses and the person's preferences about the best way to respond. Scarlett described how:

> We spent time outside of crisis really trying to consult the young person about what would be helpful ways for people to respond during a crisis to build that relationship and understanding about what's unhelpful, because we all know that a number of the young people had had very negative experiences with police or potentially with ambulance officers. And then we translated that into the individual crisis plan.

While relational and proactive ways of engaging people in conversations about planning for future crisis were underscored, our conversations continued to demonstrate the ongoing challenges involved in avoiding being inducted into dominate organisational ways of conceptualising risk.

Anti-Oppressive Approaches to Documentation

We contemplated ways of bringing a power analysis to our critical social work practice including how we engage in organisational documentation. Clinical documentation can serve to totalise the person's identity with their ascribed diagnostic categories and reinforce a deficit-focused narrative about them (Allsopp et al., 2019). We discussed how anti-oppressive documentation begins with critically thinking of the implications of the written word in mental health services. Beatrice spoke about the '*really subtle things like being really aware of language used in file notes; what's being written down and who can see the information*'. Iris expanded on this notion of anti-oppressive approaches to documentation when she shared an example where a woman she was working with had been diagnosed with Borderline Personality Disorder in the context of intimate partner violence. Iris described how because she had a well-established working relationship with the treating psychiatrist, she was able to discuss how this diagnosis might intersect with the navigation of other systems and influence the women's life. Iris said to the psychiatrist:

> I understand what you're seeing and your concerns. However, we also need to put that in context of the abuse this person's experiencing with their partner and the potential consequences of that diagnosis when this person comes into contact with other systems.

In raising these systemic implications with the multidisciplinary team and the psychiatrist, Iris explained how this contributed to documentation that reflected the person's experience outside of just the diagnosis. This example highlights how we conceptualised the social work role as going beyond anti-oppressive ways of working with individuals, to critically engage with organisational processes and procedures such as documentation.

Making Visible Coercive Practices and Advocacy

More explicit forms of resistance involved making visible the coercive practices occurring within the mental health service. The need for advocacy was central to many of our discussions to ensure the person's voice was heard in clinical processes. As Iris explained:

> I don't think social workers can take a neutral position. We need to do that extra step, which is advocacy, bringing attention to the other side that maybe the other members of the team aren't seeing. To bring to light the cultural factors or psychosocial factors that may be impacting on a person's distress.

Advocacy also involved working with the treating team to reframe what 'the problem' is, by highlighting a range of circumstances occurring in the person's life. Sometimes this involved providing more holistic information to the treating team. For example, Scarlett shared a story when she was working with a young woman who had been previously diagnosed with an intellectual disability and more recently diagnosed with 'Bipolar Disorder' by a private psychiatrist. There was pressure from the treating psychiatrist to document this diagnosis despite a lack of supporting evidence, because another psychiatrist had offered this diagnosis. Scarlett described how she, in response:

> went back to the private psychiatrist and provided all the information about other relationships in the young woman's life, how well she was doing in school, and to clarify that she was actually one of the leaders of the school.

Scarlett described that upon hearing this information, *the private psychiatrist seemed surprised.* Scarlett reflected:

> It was then I realised that private psychiatrists are often not privy to understanding the networks in the person's life, so I feel that our role is to interface between the medical system and the wider domains of the person's life to avoid misdiagnosis. He agreed to remove this diagnosis based on this new information.

On other occasions, advocacy involved social workers inviting further reflection regarding the implications of diagnosis for the person with their interdisciplinary colleagues. For example, Iris explains:

> how the symptoms that are used to diagnose Borderline Personality Disorder are very similar to those used to diagnose Complex Post-Traumatic Stress Disorder (PTSD). Complex PTSD diagnosis acknowledges this person's trauma…. It was helpful talking through the diagnosis with the team including the benefits and possible implications.

Despite an espoused commitment to 'culturally responsive' ways of working, there are ongoing tactics of colonial oppression in mental health services, particularly in situations that are deemed 'high risk'. First Nation people's resistance and reactions to the mental health system can be pathologised and seen as evidence of their 'unwellness', to justify more restrictive practices. Alyssa explained:

> As an Aboriginal person trying to access healthcare, you are already on edge about your safety in the system. Let's say you attend an ED for help but find yourself involuntarily detained, this is going to activate resistance in you where you may be yelling at medical staff. The medical staff might then deem you non-compliant and combative, which leads to being chemically restrained and seen as 'acutely unwell'. Your response to oppression is pathologised. How do you heal in a system like that?

Alyssa's analysis demonstrates opportunities for social workers to recognise how the mental health service environment is perpetuating distress and to intervene by naming the harms and challenging the psychiatrisation of resistance (Logan & Karter, 2022).

Building Bridges: Working Strategically with Multidisciplinary Colleagues to Subvert the Dominant Narrative

A consistent theme to our group discussions was the importance of working relationally not just with the people who are accessing the service, but also with our multidisciplinary colleagues. Our discussions showed the significance of building bridges of understanding between various colleagues from differing disciplines on the team, in contrast to a simplistic oppositional approach (Fook, 2016). We discussed how our advocacy efforts to ensure the voice of the person was heard would be limited without developing working relationships with the multidisciplinary team and individual team members. For example, Iris explained:

> I think both aspects of interpreting with the client and with the multidisciplinary team or the psychiatrist require a level of relationship because that's where you can communicate and have your points of view heard—when that relationship is quite strong.

Scarlett described the purpose of developing these interdisciplinary relationships *to 'be more challenging and to offer a non-biomedical point of view, in order to really try to represent their clients' perspective and realities'*. To build the foundation for these interdisciplinary relationships, it involved *'hosting other professional perspectives and discipline-specific frameworks'* (Scarlett). This hosting was done to then invite other disciplines *'to consider a social work perspective and what I was advocating for'* (Scarlett).

The social work role has sometimes been referred to as a 'facilitator' within the systems involved in a person's life (Coulter et al., 2020). However, systems work can often be uncritical in its application (Topp et al., 2021), and we spoke about recognising how systems that support people might also hold them in oppressive positions and the need to challenge the idea of 'neutrality'. We referred to the social worker role in this advocacy work as a 'translator'. As Iris describes:

> We're trying to communicate directly with the client in a way that honours their experience and in a way that reflects their experience. But we may also be trying to communicate something from the medical model. And then we are also trying to communicate back to the team from the client's perspective, in a way they're going to listen.

Being a translator involves being 'multilingual' in other disciplines' languages, while also not taking a neutral position and bringing an awareness of power. As Barbie explains:

> We know that language creates meaning, and each of the different disciplines brings their own set of bias in the room. And I wonder if it's part of your role as the social worker to understand all of those different ways in which people create meaning in mental health care and to be able to navigate through that while maintaining a focus on the person. Everybody's creating meaning around them, and so then it is our role to make sure that not only do we hear what the person is saying, but that their voice is amplified. We work with them to navigate the system, so they can continue to create their own meaning of what's happening to them rather than all these other people creating meaning for them.

To be able to be 'multilingual', we explored how to *'keep the person's meaning centred, we need to constantly navigate different knowledge systems'* (Cassidy). Cassidy characterised this as highly relational work because to truly create a sense of shared meaning that people can agree on, you have to ensure that everyone feels heard. This is occurring, however, in a context of highly unequal power dynamics, where those with more power may not be open to hearing other perspectives. Consequently, these strategic working relationships were not about minimising or collapsing an analysis of power, nor were they about assimilating psychiatric concepts into social work practice (Gomory et al., 2011); rather, they were intended to challenge the dominant medicalised narrative that develops about the person. Being a 'translator' in this sense from Cassidy's perspective means that:

> We're not a neutral party in the process. And that's where the change can come in. So we might be able to speak the medicalised language, but we have an agenda, which is about trying to even out the uneven power dynamics.

Building strategic multidisciplinary relationships was seen as a crucial aspect of social work practice, to resist clinical processes that can subjugate people's voices and lived experience expertise. Such working relationships can enhance our capacity to navigate oppressive practices and affect socially just change in mental health service provision.

Resisting Narrow Ways of Being: Celebrating Diversity and Fostering Creativity and Joy

In our discussions, we consistently returned to the challenge of resisting narrow ways of conceptualising human experience and finding possibilities for celebrating diversity and fostering joy and creativity in our work. We acknowledged how dominant notions of 'mental health' are wrapped up in notions of ideal personhood—productivity, rationality, and acceptance of the status quo. For example, the recovery concept has been co-opted by a neoliberal agenda, which can place pressure on people to enact recovery in their lives, referring to a return to pre-determined notions of 'normality' (Fullagar, 2018). We reflected on times when we have aimed to walk alongside people, to support them to resist biomedical ways of being defined, and to challenge narrow ways of thinking and being when working in mental health organisations and teams (Fullagar, 2018). The medical model focuses on eliminating 'symptoms', precluding more expansive conversations about what it might mean to have 'a life worth living' (Davidow & Mazel-Carlton, 2020). We reflected on how recovery is not a one-size-fits-all concept; and how, in fact, some people may refuse or choose to abandon the 'recovery' concept altogether, as it implies the need to accommodate to ongoing adversity (McCabe et al., 2018). We identified a key aspect of anti-oppressive practice was recognising and celebrating myriad possibilities, beyond notions of 'clinical' recovery.

We spoke about the importance of bringing a sense of creativity and joy to our interactions with people. Margaret spoke about how this was especially relevant when working with children and young people, *'that's the part where I want to be supporting them to be able to still feel joy*. Barbie described *how creativity and fun is essential, that connection across the humanness of us, workers and young people that we're working with'*. Engaging with art and creative activities in our work may enable people to reconnect and make visible their knowledges that have been subjugated by biomedical paradigms (Tseris et al., 2024). Sarah noted that social work can move beyond narrow biomedical preoccupations and find creative ways of working:

> Just getting past this idea that we're there to eliminate so-called symptoms. People might actually deserve to have meaningful, joyful lives.

Working in creative and joyful ways is another example of resistance to a pathologising, totalising, and deficit focus, to instead focus on a person's life beyond the diagnosis. In this way, 'creativity can create a space for considering other possible worlds, beyond the status quo' (Tseris et al., 2024, p. 165). We also spoke about the importance of being on the look-out for hope and inviting hopeful conversations despite the challenges being experienced. Frankie explained how she has intentionally sought to:

> Notice beauty and notice hope, because I know I have fallen into traps before—there's so much injustice that it might seem almost disrespectful to bring beauty or hope into the conversation; the idea that a person might find it dismissive if I bring us back to what they find hopeful, or the beauty that they're noticing. I've fallen into that trap before. But it's an ethical imperative for us to be doing that, especially in these times, although not in a way that minimises someone's pain. I have always found this so challenging, particularly when meeting with people who are incredibly far from my social, economic and political experience.

This is a way of working that aims to acknowledge that people are not reducible to the harms they have experienced within societies and systems (Tseris et al., 2024) and to recognise resistance in ways that amplify the dignity and skills of people who have survived oppression (Reynolds, 2020). In contrast to a simplistic approach to 'noticing strengths', Frankie noted that attention to context and complexity is needed, in order to avoid the hazard of minimising injustices and violations. In this way, we understood that our social work practice has a role to play in both acknowledging and addressing the oppressive social structures that perpetuate distress, and at the same time, engaging with generative practices that open possibilities for hope, and creating space for people to engage with joy and to live their preferred lives. This aimed to provide a contrast to a symptom-orientation, which is centred narrowly and pessimistically on eliminating the so-called dysfunctions within people, leading to prescriptive pathways and definitions of 'recovery'. As social workers who are located within and navigating oppressive systems, such practices aspired to be more than an intellectual critique of such systems; to move 'beyond protesting the current circumstances, to creating new conditions of possibility' (Ben-Moshe, 2018, p.353).

Conclusion

Enacting critical approaches to mental health social work practice within biomedical organisations is complex and yet remains under-explored and unarticulated in research and scholarship. This chapter demonstrates the ongoing ethical challenges social workers face in finding ways to navigate oppressive practices. It explores the sometimes small and other times, more explicit ways that social workers have tried to engage in practices of resistance, to move beyond the 'buzzwords' and find ways to challenge risk-adverse paradigms, including the role of advocacy. While we discussed the role of social workers as 'translator' between the person, the multidisciplinary team, and system, this role is not neutral and requires an astute analysis of the matrix of unequal power relationships. This chapter has aimed to unpack these ethical challenges in order to inspire further critical reflection and collective discussions to develop social work's professional accountability in response to oppressive practices within the neoliberal, biomedical regime.

References

Allsopp, K., Read, J., Corcoran, R., & Kinderman, P. (2019). Heterogeneity in psychiatric diagnostic classification. *Psychiatry Research, 279*, 15–22.

Askew, D., Brady, K., Mukandi, B., Singh, D., Sinha, S., Brough, M., & Bond, C. J. (2020). Closing the gap between rhetoric and practice in strengths-based approaches to Indigenous public health: A qualitative study. *Australian and New Zealand Journal of Public Health, 44*(2), 102–105. https://doi.org/10.1111/1753-6405.12953

Ben-Moshe, L. (2018). Dis-epistemologies of abolition. *Critical Criminology, 26*(3), 341–355.

Brown, C. (2024). Reframing trauma through social justice resisting the politics of mainstream trauma discourse. Taylor & Francis.

Brown, C. (2021). Critical clinical social work and the neoliberal constraints on social justice in mental health. *Research on Social Work Practice, 31*(6), 644–652.

Brown, C. (2020). Feminist narrative therapy and complex trauma: Critical clinical work with women diagnosed as "borderline". In C. Brown & J. McDonald (Eds.), *Critical clinical social work: Counterstorying for social justice* (pp. 82–109). Canadian Scholars' Press.

Carey, M., & Foster, V. (2011). Introducing 'deviant'social work: Contextualising the limits of radical social work whilst understanding (fragmented) resistance within the social work labour process. *British Journal of Social Work, 41*(3), 576–593.

Coulter, S., Houston, S., Mooney, S., Devaney, J., & Davidson, G. (2020). Attaining theoretical coherence within relationship-based practice in child and family social work: The systemic perspective. *British Journal of Social Work, 50*(4), 1219–1237.

Davidow, S., & Mazel-Carlton, C. (2020). The "alternatives to suicide" approach: A decade of lessons learned. In A. Page & W. Stritzke (Eds.), *Alternatives to suicide* (pp. 179–199). Academic Press.

Davidson, G., Brophy, L., Campbell, J., Farrell, S. J., Gooding, P., & O'Brien, A.-M. (2016). An international comparison of legal frameworks for supported and substitute decision-making in mental health services. *International Journal of Law and Psychiatry, 44*, 30–40.

Fook, J. (2016). *Social work: A critical approach to practice*. Sage.

Fullagar, S. (2018). Foucauldian theory. In B. M. Z. Cohen (Ed.), *Routledge international handbook of critical mental health* (pp. 39–45). Routledge.

Gomory, T., Wong, S. E., Cohen, D., & Lacasse, J. R. (2011). Clinical social work and the biomedical industrial complex. *Journal of Sociology and Socia Welfare, 38*, 135–165.

Gray, M. (2011). Back to basics: A critique of the strengths perspective in social work. *Families in Society, 92*(1), 5–11.

Greenslade, L., McAuliffe, D., & Chenoweth, L. (2015). Social workers' experiences of covert workplace activism. *Australian Social Work, 68*(4), 422–437.

Johnstone, M., & Lee, E. (2024). Repositioning our understanding of trauma through the lens of epistemic injustice and hermeneutic omissions. In C. Brown (Ed.), *Reframing trauma through social justice* (pp. 43–56). Routledge.

Kelly, C., & Chapman, C. (2015). Adversarial allies: Care, harm, and resistance in the helping professions. *Journal of Progressive Human Services, 26*(1), 46–66.

Laing, M., & Maylea, C. (2018). A conceptual framework for taking subversive social work into the classroom. *Advances in Social Work and Welfare Education, 20*(2), 23–30.

Logan, J., & Karter, J. M. (2022). Psychiatrization of resistance: The co-option of consumer, survivor, and ex-patient movements in the global south. *Frontiers in Sociology, 7*, 784390.

Manchester, R. (2015). Towards critical mental health social work: Learning from critical psychiatry and psychiatry survivors. *Critical and Radical Social Work, 3*(1), 149–154. https://doi.org/10.1332/204986015X14225321433339

Maylea, C. H. (2017). A rejection of involuntary treatment in mental health social work. *Ethics and Social Welfare, 11*(4), 336–352.

McCabe, R., Whittington, R., Cramond, L., & Perkins, E. (2018). Contested understandings of recovery in mental health. *Journal of Mental Health, 27*(5), 475–481.

Oaten, A., Jordan, A., Chandler, A., & Marzetti, H. (2022). Suicide prevention as biopolitical surveillance: A critical analysis of UK suicide prevention policies. *Critical Social Policy, 43*(4), 654–675.

Portelli, J., & Eizadirad, A. (2018). Subversion in education: Common misunderstandings and myths. *International Journal of Critical Pedagogy, 9*(1), 53–72.

Reid, K., Olsen, A., Farwa, A., & Wyder, M. (in press). *"It's a relational approach, first and foremost, with the whole system": Social work perspectives on recovery-oriented approaches with children and their families*. Feminism and Psychology.

Reid, K., Olsen, A., Farwa, A., Dalziel, M., & Wyder, M. (2024). The translation of recovery-oriented social work practice in child and youth mental health: A scoping review. *The British Journal of Social Work, 54*(6), 2506–2525.

Reid, K., & Alford, J. (2023). Empowerment or holding the child responsible? an Australian recovery-oriented mental health policy analysis. *British Journal of Social Work, 53*(5), 2860–2877.

Reynolds, V. (2020). Trauma and resistance: 'Hang time' and other innovative responses to oppression, violence and suffering. *Journal of Family Therapy, 42*(3), 347–364.

Ross, D. (2020). Toward coercion free, trauma-informed care in Australian adult mental health services: Strategies for social workers. *Social Work in Mental Health, 18*(5), 536–553.

Topp, S. M., Schaaf, M., Sriram, V., Scott, K., Dalglish, S. L., Nelson, E. M., et al. (2021). Power analysis in health policy and systems research: a guide to research conceptualisation. *BMJ Global Health, 6*(11), e007268.

Tseris, E. (2019). *Trauma, women's mental health, and social justice: pitfalls and possibilities*. Routledge.

Tseris, E., Franks, S., & Hart, E. B. (2024). *Psychiatric oppression in women's lives: creative resistance and collective dissent*. Palgrave Macmillan.

Chapter 5
Exploring Opportunities for Community Work and Transforming Systems in Mental Health Social Work: Expanding Our Gaze

Across the globe, people with lived experiences of psychiatric diagnoses are critiquing the limitations of biomedical constructions of human experience, and engaging in community building as a radical form of resistance and liberatory world-making in response to the harms and limitations of mainstream mental health service provision. In this chapter, we foreground the possibilities of working collectively with groups and in solidarity with communities as part of everyday mental health social work practice, in identifying and responding to the socio-political contexts of distress. Examples of practice that emerged from a cooperative inquiry research process on mental health social work and social justice are discussed (see Chap. 1). Mental health social work is informed by iterative and nuanced analyses of social conditions, based upon building relationships of care and solidarity with people experiencing distress. The cooperative inquiry revealed that some of us have worked in situations that have allowed space for responding to these analyses through collective practice in groups or community work. Unfortunately, in contemporary times, such approaches are being crowded out by an ever-increasing focus on 'clinical' mental health practice, based upon the notion of 'expert' professionals involved in 'treating illness' (Chapman et al., 2020). The elevation of individual-focused approaches is evident in the growing emphasis on clinical approaches in mental health, for example, the growth of social workers in private practice (Papadopoulos & Maylea, 2020). Chaps. 3 and 4 explored how social workers grapple with a social analysis of power in 'clinical' spaces, and at times, find generative opportunities to resist biomedical power. In addition to this, it is important that social work critiques the now widely accepted notion that working with individuals is the 'gold standard'—perhaps the only legitimate approach in mental health practice—an idea which has gained prominence in the context of the neoliberalisation of mental health (Brown, 2021). Due to the ease of measuring individual 'clinical' approaches according to neoliberal standards, such as Key Performance Indicators (Pease, 2020; Strier & Bershtling, 2016), a collective or community-led approach may be

L. Whitaker et al., *Social Work in the Mental Health Field*, SpringerBriefs in Social Work, https://doi.org/10.1007/978-3-032-08306-7_5

viewed as a less 'valuable' or less 'legitimate' approach in the mental health field, but we argue that such a positioning needs to be challenged.

A second key focus in this chapter is on the opportunities and complexities involved in working towards meaningful systems change and transformative paradigm shifts in the mental health field. Given the constraints on social work practice within biomedical and neoliberal workplaces, we were interested to explore if and how it might be possible to contribute towards re-shaping the systems in which we work and re-considering our ways of working within and beyond such systems. The questions we considered included: Is it possible to enable people to access support and resources outside the mainstream mental health system, in ways that can better address the social determinants of distress and prevent the harms of coercive interventions? How can we strategically use the resources of a biomedically focused organisation towards enacting a more expansive approach? Is leaving an oppressive workplace a pathway that can or should be considered, in order to find a different context where it might be more possible to enact social justice values? Through these questions, we attempted to explore the opportunities that exist in mental health social work to resist, even in small ways (Egan et al., 2024), a diagnostic approach to making sense of human experience, and instead to explore contextualised, collective, ethical, and politicised ways of responding with people experiencing distress and difference.

Why Work with Communities?

Working collectively and collaboratively with communities can provide opportunities to acknowledge and address the intrinsic connections between social inequalities and distress (Karban, 2017). It has a well-established, if somewhat oblique, history in social work (Howard & Rawsthorne, 2020), in extending social work beyond the constraints of what is possible when working with individuals, for example, the limitations that can be present in private practice contexts. As noted by Beatrice:

> If you're employed in private practice, you might not be able to do the work of connecting people—that kind of collaborative approach.

In our discussions, we explored the often complex—and frequently less visible—skills that are involved in community work. When we turn our attention to working in relationally and collectively, outside of a 'treatment' paradigm, possibilities can emerge to disrupt the harmful professional agendas and power imbalances between workers and those on the receiving end of services (Whitaker et al., 2021). This involves understanding the limitations of centring a 'professional expert', and challenging the idea that distress is evidence of 'individual pathology'. Consequently, we can take steps to challenge diagnostically-oriented responses to distress, working in ways that provide space for people and communities to have more power, while also starting to address the social drivers of distress. For example, working outside an 'individual treatment' paradigm challenges the isolation and disconnection that can happen in therapeutic spaces, leading to opportunities for people with lived experiences of injustice and violence to join together, learn from each other, and experience solidarity. This in itself is political work (Salter, 2021), which can enable social workers to move beyond the limits of rhetorical commitments to social justice and towards practices that enable us to make connections between structural and institutional oppressions and 'personal' experiences of distress (Parker, 2017). We have found that working with groups and communities enables important opportunities. These include:

- ***Disrupting notions of individual pathology***, since connecting with others can reveal patterns of power and enable unjust systems to be made more visible. When people connect and share experiences, a structural power analysis becomes more likely, rather than a gaze on personal 'deficits' (Salter, 2021). As noted by Barbie, this disrupts the paternalistic assumption that an individual should simply '*work on their individual recovery'*.
- ***Engaging in consciousness-raising***, so that the status quo can be challenged. For example, when working with women who have experienced violence, the sharing of lived experiences enables the context of patriarchal power to become clearer (Tseris et al., 2024). Once this has happened, women's knowledges regarding how they are reclaiming their lives after violence can become more visible, so the focus of the group can re-orientate away from imposing professional knowledges, to sharing knowledges as a collective (Muller, 2005). As Beatrice noted, the socio-political drivers are often overlooked within an individual 'treatment' approach:

> *Domestic violence might be really impacting on a person's situation. And yet, when we're looking from a biomedical view, we're looking at the symptoms and the person, not necessarily taking the context into account.*

This example demonstrates that through bringing people together, there are opportunities to collectively identify the power structures that perpetuate distress.

- ***Making the connections between social contexts and wellbeing*** more evident, thus questioning the diagnostic paradigm of distress. This follows on from our discussion regarding the value of attending to the politics of experience, in Chap. 3. As social workers, we are attuned to the ways in which social contexts can lead to significant distress, and we discussed opportunities to use the resources of a mental health organisation to make such contexts visible. For example, Cassidy described how 'mental health awareness-raising' can be re-framed away from approaches that bolster a diagnostic framing of human experience, and instead an organisation could be encouraged to mark International Trans Day of Visibility (TDoV), as a way of highlighting queer pride and social change. This example demonstrates the possibility of carving out spaces within mental health organisations to call out injustices and to stand in solidarity with people experiencing violence and exclusion. Such approaches differ from a traditional mental health paradigm, which conceals the political contexts of people's lives through the language of 'disorder' and places the 'problem' in the person. In other words, if we are only seeing people for individual 'treatment' or 'therapy', we are privatising social issues and power relations. Crucially, we also discussed how such processes should not be approached superficially, as a box-ticking inclusion exercise; rather, social work practice in this space requires a genuinely relational, iterative, and participatory approach (Howard & Rawsthorne, 2020). The pitfalls of tokenism are discussed in more detail later in this chapter.

– ***Supporting people to connect around shared experiences and knowledges***, rather than experiencing ongoing social exclusion and discrimination. For example, Sarah described what becomes possible when people who have survived violence and injustice are able to meet and share experiences:

> Taking the focus away from the individual to the collective and then developing into possibilities to learn from each other as well. There is so much evidence regarding the negative impacts of isolation and disconnection on levels of distress. Are we suggesting that people keep coming to therapy until they don't feel isolated? A therapeutic paradigm is not actually addressing isolation or discrimination.

Despite its potential, the cooperative inquiry also explored how it is important not to idealise community work and assume its inherent connections to social justice, nor to position it as fundamentally collaborative, without power imbalances. Below we outline several key challenges that were revealed in our research.

Engaging with the Complexities and Potential Neoliberal Pitfalls of Community Work

Despite the benefits and possibilities of group and community work, there are also many potential pitfalls. Our research explored the pressures faced by social workers, for example, narrow approaches to measuring outcomes and the pressure to adopt a fast pace. We also critiqued risk-oriented ways of understanding groups and communities who are experiencing injustices, inequalities, violence, and distress. We discussed how engaging with such challenges is important, as we do not intend to draw a neat binary between individual work and group/community work. Just as 'clinical' work is rife with pathologising discourses, community work can become enmeshed in neoliberal, risk-averse, and biomedical paradigms, if we are not developing responses that are accountable to the people with whom we work and attuned to these hazards.

Managing Competing Agendas

There can be immense pressures on social workers to meet the Key Performance Indicators (KPIs) of an organisation and promote the needs of a service, rather than the priorities of a community. A stark example is using community events to primarily increase the visibility of a service, rather than responding to what the community identifies as important. This is relevant in the context of neoliberal service provision, where services are constantly competing for funding (Finley et al., 2012), which can act as a significant distraction from the priority of working relationally with people and communities. Here, we can see a misapplication of a community-oriented paradigm and an unethical use of resources to bolster organisational agendas. As noted by Cassidy:

> For events that are labelled as 'community events', sometimes organisations can prioritise relationships with other organisations and services, over the priorities of the community itself. I've noticed that services can fail to do any consultation with the actual community and just put on an event, invite a bunch of services and then have no-one from the community turn up—which is a waste of resources, to be honest.

Resisting the Pressure to Adopt a Fast Pace

Social workers may experience pressures from funding arrangements to achieve outcomes quickly, in ways that do not involve genuine engagement with community members, nor create meaningful opportunities for social inclusion; instead, the event becomes a mere 'box-ticking' exercise. As described by Margaret:

> Co-design just takes longer because it involves different ways of communicating … not everyone sitting on an online meeting, for example. And I wonder if sometimes in organisations it's just hard to sit with slow.

Following the slower pace required for meaningful relationship building is therefore a relevant strategy in enacting resistance to institutional neoliberal expectations (Strier & Bershtling, 2016).

Challenging the Expectation to Provide Pre-Determined Outcomes

There can be additional pressures to 'prove' the benefits of community work in highly concrete outcomes, and to show immediate benefits, which can be distilled into the requirements of funding bodies. This is particularly problematic, because community engagement takes time, and involves an iterative and relational approach. Our research explored how social workers, therefore, can articulate the importance of a more participatory approach. As noted by Frankie, an individualised approach to service provision may not be culturally safe for First Nations women who have experienced incarceration, racism, and intergenerational trauma, and an alternative approach needs to be put forward in order for funders and colleagues in multidisciplinary teams to understand the benefits and to provide resources:

> We were having a barbeque every Friday, so first the responses [on the broader team] were, 'Oh, what for?' and I responded, 'I don't know—I don't know what we're doing yet'. My rationale was that women were saying that they don't want to be sitting in front of some-

> body as a client in a mainstream service, because that feels like too much. So, I just proposed a Friday barbeque. And there was something in not overthinking it and not having something necessarily the way that mainstream health services around us wanted us to—it was just a space.

This example demonstrates the benefits of challenging a 'search for certainty' by defining what the service is 'delivering', as community work requires an open space in which community members define the purpose of the interaction over time. This stands in stark contrast to the 'clinical' roll-out of pre-defined interventions in community settings.

Resisting a Clinical Paradigm

We discussed expectations to engage in overly prescriptive practices (for example, requirements for participants to register for an event by providing their personal details; placing limitations and rules around friendships formed during community gatherings), with such requirements often based on the biomedical assumption that connecting people is 'risky'. As discussed by Scarlett:

> Groupwork has become sanitized as an approach whereby the expert delivers psychoeducation to the client to compensate for their 'deficits'. Often this approach to groupwork is informed by the idea that we have to teach individuals emotional regulation skills to enable them to better manage their mental health. Psychoeducation is a key part of the neoliberal agenda, where individuals are expected to learn mindfulness strategies to self-regulate more efficiently and effectively. Over the years I've done a different kind of group work, which involves bringing people together… to connect people around experiences of injustice and shared knowledge. Without clinically defined outcomes, it is almost seen as dangerous, to bring young people together around shared experiences when they're supposedly 'clinically unwell'.

Margaret further explained '*sometimes one of the worries about groups especially is that people will come together and there will be kind of 'emotional dysregulation'*. We explored how social workers, therefore, need strategies to articulate the purpose of group and community work, without centring themselves as 'the expert', finding ways to deftly challenge the barriers to collective responses to distress and to question problematic 'risk management' practices and the pathologisation of distress.

Questioning Standardisation

There can be pressures to utilise rigid and standardised protocols, which mimic 'clinical' work with individuals, re-inscribing the professional as the 'expert', in ways that can stop us from working in participatory and iterative ways. Such approaches can be seen within many 'psychoeducation' and even 'art therapy' groups, which sometimes follow a manual, and keep people in the position of a recipient of 'care', thus retaining the norms of professional power. In this way, groupwork acts as an intervention to resolve individual 'deficits', similarly to clinical practice. As noted by Scarlett, *'it's almost like we have to define what the purpose is, before we actually bring people together'*. Even within non-manualised groups (where workers are not expected to adhere strictly to a therapeutic protocol), there can still be expectations on workers to focus much too heavily on 'content' and 'outcomes', rather than processes and relationships. As noted by Margaret:

> What was frustrating was doing all of that quality improvement documentation from the start and having to decide on the outcomes of the group before you've actually done the group. Which leads to focusing on the content of the group, as opposed to the power of getting people together and having it be more of an organic, client-led process.

Here, we can see a clinical paradigm drifting into community work, seriously undermining an iterative and community-led approach.

Skills in Resisting Biomedical Neoliberalism

We discussed how biomedical understandings intersect with neoliberal ideology, by positioning people as responsible for adapting to unjust social environments, distracting social workers from the need for social change, building community, and addressing social exclusion. In response to these significant challenges, the research explored the understandings and practices that can make a difference when working with groups and communities, considering points of resistance in response to neoliberal and biomedical assumptions (Strier & Bershtling, 2016). This section will explore how we can re-orientate to alternative understandings of risk, value opportunities for collectivising, and re-imagine social work in a community context, to bring a curious, contextual, and relational approach.

Re-orienting Understandings of Risk in Community Work

As previously explored in the book, it has been widely recognised that mental health practice is increasingly characterised by risk aversion, which places significant constraints on creative, collective, and community-led responses to social inequalities. The preoccupation with risk has significant implications for professional autonomy and the ability of social workers to maintain a commitment to social change (Callahan, in Clarke & Morley, 2022). At the same time, mental health workers often privilege risk aversion due to fears about the public scrutiny that may arise, if they are deemed to have failed to manage 'risk'. In this way, the conduct of both people receiving mental health services and workers is placed under intense surveillance, albeit in diverse ways (Watts & Hodgson, 2019). Beatrice noted that such perspectives lead to a very concerning picture, whereby workers are:

> Thinking about themselves and their own accountability: Will I have to front up to the Coroner's court? That's the focus, rather than: Is this person going to be OK? And what's the very best for them?

This emphasis on risk aversion may go some way towards explaining how managerialist and 'evidence-based' practice agendas have increasingly privileged individual-focused approaches, and the role of mental health organisations in keeping people apart from one another. Clinical and manualised treatment approaches can lead to social disconnection and de-politicised practices, which places the 'problem' within the person, as noted by Margaret:

> What's the risk of not getting people together and people continuing to be more isolated and siloed?

In contrast to biomedical approaches regarding the 'risky' emotions arising in groupwork contexts, there are opportunities to work in a way that fosters collective knowledge-building and recognising resistance, as Scarlett discussed:

> There's some real power in moving away from individual to collective stories. Our approach was not merely to invite people to reiterate stories of violence, but to bring their knowledge to more broadly explore the tactics of abuse: How do they operate in women's lives? Asking questions that drew forth their agency in terms of how they've responded, rather than only what happened to them. We're trying to make visible these acts of resistance that they've already taken. To stand together in this resistance to violence against women.

Here, we see opportunities to contest the notion that collective emotions are 'risky', including anger-eliminativism—the view that anger is a negative emotion, which should be suppressed and minimised (Gasdaglis, 2025). Instead, anger can be understood as a meaningful response to being violated and experiencing oppression. It can speak to a sense of wrong-doing and social injustice. We discussed together how the focus on eliminating risk is problematic, as traditional risk assessment tools are connected to an illusion of certainty and objectivity—an unrealistic and unhelpful goal within the context of complex human and social experiences (Pease, 2020). In short, we will never be able to arrive at a situation of 'no risk'. Indeed, a focus on calculating risk through actuarial risk assessment tools can distract from a range of other social work understandings and contributions (Clarke & Morley, 2022). This is reflected in Beatrice's discussion about the need to move beyond a preoccupation with risk assessment towards walking alongside people, identifying the numerous skills that are evident in their lives:

> So it shifts it from saying, 'Oh, we've got to predict. Everything's going to be risky, and we've got to manage it', to be saying, 'Actually, we're here because we're working with people, and how do we actually listen to what people find helpful and go with them?'

A biomedical paradigm, which locates risk within individuals, can therefore be challenged, through critiquing the assumption that professionals are the only people who can understand risk. This involves privileging lived experience expertise, as well as noticing the existing connections and networks in people's lives, which are often de-valued or ignored by mental health workers. As discussed by Iris, working in a small community setting:

> I felt really confident that the community knew how to support each other. And I also recognised the community's ability and often a family's ability to manage some of that risk too. I think sometimes we view it as though it has to be a service that is the expert in managing risk, but often people have really incredible skills in managing risk themselves.

Taking these relational and community-led approaches therefore involves a decentring of professional power, and attention to a more expansive set of possibilities for understanding and responding to distress and injustice.

Valuing Opportunities for Collectivising

We discussed opportunities that are available for social work to resist dominant medicalised narratives and engage in political action. For example, Scarlett described her experience facilitating a group for women survivors of gendered violence who had been labelled with mental health diagnoses. Multiple conversations with individual women led to a consideration about the connections and shared experiences between women in the local area and the possibility of forming a group. The group disrupted traditional ideas about what is knowledge (medical understandings of distress; diagnostic assessment) and who holds the knowledge (professionals). Collective discussions and actions among the women enabled a structural analysis of power, challenging dominant narratives regarding women's 'mental health' towards a recognition of patriarchal power. The group processes also illuminated how women were already actively resisting both gendered violence and pathologising understandings of distress:

> This groupwork approach was really about drawing out the local knowledge of women about gendered oppressions. There was such power in the group members finding their own words or images to name oppression. Each week we were exploring women's knowledge about how tactics of abuse and control operated in their relationships, but we also explored those broader discourses that support violence against women. Obviously, their mental health experiences were in relation to these other tactics of abuse and control in their lives, so we weren't just working on their mental health 'symptoms'. Women started voicing their concerns about the impacts of violence on women and their mental health and identified that this was a shared issue, so the groupwork facilitation was really about linking woman's shared experiences of oppression to broader societal concerns. Shared knowledge about how they were reclaiming their lives from these tactics went beyond coping strategies, it was more about decisions they made or forms of resistance that they were demonstrating. We then started attending political marches together. What started as a personal issue led to a collective concern about violence against women and collective political action.

Importantly, Scarlett noted that the sharing of experiences is not about collapsing differences, but rather, valuing multiplicity:

> Inviting people to share their stories in a way that does not create a hierarchy of 'right' and 'wrong', or a binary of 'recovered' or 'not recovered', because everyone's different.

Even when tasked with the requirement to run a psychoeducation group, which may be quite narrow in scope, Scarlett explored how social workers can take opportunities to incorporate a more politicised understanding of mental health:

> We could subvert some of the activities within a manualised group, for example, in discussing 'self-regulation', we could draw on people's knowledge about what gets in the way of 'self-regulation' and then to question the concept itself. What are some societal challenges? We could then de-construct the broader context of people's lives.

This example illuminates how social workers need not be defined and limited by the setting in which we are situated, but can enact social justice values, even within hostile and unjust environments (Fook, 2016)—using creativity and considering the ways in which the resources and agendas of an organisation can be re-oriented towards addressing the social drivers of distress and exploring how people resist oppression.

Re-imagining the Role of Social Work Away from 'Therapeutic Expert'

Our discussions reflected opportunities to re-conceptualise mental health social work as a role that is focused on resourcing connections, rather than leading processes. This is sometimes de-valued and less visible work and requires us to think differently about our role, outside the scope of a 'therapeutic or clinical expert'. An example, described by Cassidy, reveals the skills involved in understanding what people are seeking, supporting connections to relevant community resources, and unobtrusively fostering those connections, through de-centring professional expertise:

> Some of the best community development work I've been involved in has been about services getting out of the way. For example, here is a group of young First Nations people; here is First Nations Elder who is offering cultural knowledge—let's just provide resources to make this happen. Let's get a bus, offer it to all to these young people and then take them to the Elder and the Elder can do this workshop, then we take them back. There's a bit of humility involved in that kind of work, because it's got nothing to do with us as an organisation. We have access to the resources, so we're giving people that path that they wouldn't have had an option for otherwise. It's much quieter, I'd say. And you know, it's not appropriate to be taking photos in a lot of those situations and posting it all over social media. The impact was significant and it meant that those ten young people had access to cultural support in a way they hadn't before. And it builds. But it's interesting going through the process of realising, 'Oh, I'm not needed'. Just taking a step back like that can be hard sometimes.

This is an important illustration of the skill of 'doing yourself out of a job'. However, herein lies a tension. The subtlety and humility of the practice are important, and yet, it is this very subtlety that may position community-led approaches as less legitimate than a 'clinical' paradigm, leaving them open to neoliberal cost-cutting measures.

Despite its marginalisation as an approach in the mental health field, fostering meaningful connections with the existing networks within a community—in contrast to a siloed and generic roll-out of mental health services without due attention to local contexts—requires nuanced skills, thoughtfulness, and resources, as noted by Iris:

> I started to develop relationships with the local NGO hub. I attended community meetings with other services in the community that would meet regularly to talk about what they were providing and what the gaps were and what the community really needed. The organisation I worked in started to recognise the value in these partnerships.

In another example, Beatrice discussed that in addition to connecting people to community resources, social work involves understanding and working with *'people's networks and communities around them, fitting in with people'* rather than expecting people to 'fit in' with services. This can create a much more meaningful response, moving past the assumption that 'the service knows best', which sometimes leads to a situation whereby people are blamed for not taking up mainstream services, without due consideration that a service might be unhelpful, or indeed, harmful.

Alyssa discussed the importance of connecting to both community *and* Country, drawing on First Nations knowledges:

> Every community is different; when I focus on connection to community and connection to Country I'm focusing on the strengths; let's focus on things that can keep you well, the strengths of our people. Rather than focusing on some more mainstream, Westernized interventions. So, if you're a saltwater person, do you need to go down to the beach and put your feet in the ocean? If you're a freshwater person but you live in the middle of the city, where is the closest river you can go to? The idea is to recreate that grounding in Mother Earth.

Here, we can see a privileging First Nations knowledges of social and emotional wellbeing, and considering what it might actually mean to work in a 'holistic' way—not only fostering relationships with others but also considering the ecological determinants of health in colonial contexts and the 'direct link between land, place and mental wellness (or a lack thereof)' (Josewski et al., 2023. p.1).

A Humble and Relational Approach

Our discussions highlighted the need to work relationally and respectfully with communities, rather than imposing pre-determined goals and structures. This requires a change of pace and challenging neoliberal constructions of time, where outcomes need to happen quickly (Mehrotra, 2023). It also requires humility, a willingness to learn, and being comfortable with uncertainty. As Cassidy said:

> We need to work at the pace of communities, rather than the pace of KPIs, and to ask the question: how will this support service users or potential service users? In my role I've been able to advocate and implement more co-design, so involving people with lived experience, whether that's clients or staff, to decide what kind of events to run for particular communities. That makes a huge difference in the quality of the work.

Although co-design is sometimes watered down into a once-off tokenistic engagement with community members (McKercher, 2020), meaningful co-design processes are iterative and flexible, as part of an ongoing conversation and commitment to learning with communities:

> It wasn't pre-planned. I started working in that community just thinking it was going to be very similar to the ways that I had worked in other communities, and then I realised it was quite different. It just evolved over time and involved following the lead of the community and what was coming up within the community. It naturally progressed as issues would come up (Iris).

Scarlett also spoke about being open to the priorities and perspectives of a group of women with experiences of mental distress and gendered violence in order to develop much more meaningful responses, rather than a set of pre-determined, worker-led actions:

> We followed the direction of the group and they really wanted to take a political stand. So I think it is about supporting those relationships beyond the agency and not centralising your role in people's lives, but you're actually building networks between people who have some shared experiences and knowledge.

Scarlett described the value of peer-led and co-facilitated groups, and the immense value of ensuring people who have direct lived experiences are actively involved in the leadership and development of groups, while being fairly remunerated for this work. Being aware of the widespread co-option and tokenism of peer work within mental health services, this involves critical reflection throughout the process, including looking for opportunities to collaborate with peer workers to co-design right from the beginning as opposed to adding on lived experience perspectives later. Although time-intensive, what results from this work is more sustained and meaningful forms of engagement with community members, deeper relationships, and more transformative social change, rather than tokenism.

Beyond co-design, transformative practices can happen when as social workers we not only 'go into' communities as outsiders, but we ourselves are part of a community, so that we bring experiential expertise to inform our work. This is about breaking down a binary between 'workers' and 'people with lived experiences'. For example, Cassidy spoke about the value of working with LGBTQ+ communities, as a member of the LGBTQ+ community:

> My main experience is working in LGBTQ+ spaces, and consultation and co-design in those spaces. I'm part of the community as well, and having a worker who identifies with a particular community will have a significant impact on the kind of work being done. Our lived experience gives us insight into how to approach community and how to run a group that is accessible, which sounds simple but is not at all.

This work challenges taken-for-granted assumptions about the perceived separateness of workers and people receiving services (Sinclair et al., 2023). While collapsing differences is neither realistic nor helpful, a more contextualised and nuanced approach to understanding boundaries can open up different ways of relating (O'leary et al., 2013).

When we don't have direct lived experiences to inform our work, there is a lot to consider in how we build relationships with and work in solidarity with people who have experiential expertise, ensuring we are accountable in our work. For example, Iris talked about an example of working with a community and resisting a 'psycho-education' response, which would position her as the 'expert'. Instead, Iris took the position of a co-learner:

> The thing that stood out to me was how the community really supported each other, and there were other things that supported the person outside of a mental health service. It was a really interesting experience for me in adjusting my practice and considering what was going to be helpful for people, acknowledging the way they viewed their own experiences. It wasn't based on us being the experts and knowing what was right for them. It was a really good space to work in, where people actually started to communicate what they needed and what they thought was helpful. The idea that 'mental illness' is actually socially constructed, that's something I thought about a lot, working in this community. It was really clear to me that people had a very different views of their experience—I don't think I ever used labels or diagnosis when I was talking to people because it just wasn't something that really resonated with them. I feel like I learnt so much through that experience.

In these examples, we can see that working with groups and communities opens up many possibilities beyond the bounds of individualised, clinical approaches to mental health. This challenges an unhelpful hierarchy between the perceived legitimacy of individual 'clinical' work and more collective responses to distress. Through sharing and co-analysing detailed experiences from practice, the skills involved in working with communities were made more visible. In addition, the examples illuminate how much pressure there is on social workers in a contemporary context to comply with risk-averse, manualised, and quantifiable paradigms. While there is no set formula or guaranteed approach, and the examples demonstrated varying impacts and change, our research process highlighted the relevance of a collective critical reflection on the question: 'How can I challenge and change structures when it is those same structures which employ me?' (Fook, 2016, p.204).

Beyond Complicity: Working Towards a Paradigm Shift

In the next section of this chapter, we share reflections arising from the cooperative inquiry research process, regarding the actions that social workers can take in contributing to change within biomedically oriented organisations, towards fostering more expansive, relational, and politically attuned approaches. We argue that the status quo of Western mental health organisations is not immutable; rather, there are opportunities for social work to expand our gaze beyond the current system, by adopting a 'resistant imagination' (Medina, 2013, p.299), finding pragmatic—and sometimes fragmented—opportunities for resistance (Carey & Foster, 2011), and maintaining a curiosity about how the resources of an organisation can be used differently (Cohen, 1998). Below, we share examples of how strategic, reflective, and collective approaches have made a difference. Many of these ideas resonate with and extend the critical practices that were described in Chap. 4's exploration of navigating oppressive systems.

Finding Points of Resistance within Biomedical Settings

Sometimes, we can use the purported values of an organisation as strategy of resistance, using an organisation's rhetorical commitments as a justification for offering different approaches, pathways, and options, beyond a clinical framework. For example, Frankie discussed the way in which she advocated for changes in service provision, based on the wording used within the policies and procedures of her organisation:

> At our organisation we talk about being 'trauma-informed' and wanting to 'hear client voices and lived experience'. So, the most powerful way for me to get something off the ground is to actually get information from the people that we're supporting—using the purported values and the ethics of the service as an advocacy tool to say, 'You've said it is your priority to listen to women. The women are asking for X, Y and Z. Let's go'. They haven't usually been able to decline it, because it's actually in the policies.

We also discussed how we can move beyond *critiquing* the biomedical approach, which can encourage us to take on a defensive position about our role on a multidisciplinary team, towards a more *generative* approach to describing what it is we have to contribute as mental health social workers. This is not about reaching a place of problematic certainty or professional hubris, but rather, is about over time gaining skills and building cross-disciplinary relationships in order to clearly and confidently articulate the benefits of a holistic perspective and social work practice contributions, in order to put forward a different perspective, as outlined by Iris:

> That is sometimes the complexity of our work—managing different relationships, and the different lenses through which people are seeing the same person and maybe the same experiences, but understanding it very differently. Even though I'm not a doctor, and I'm not necessarily assessing their diagnosis or prescribing medication, I have a valuable input. Often, I knew the clients and the community a lot better than the psychiatrist did, who sometimes only came in once every three months. So that gave me more confidence. I started seeing part of my role as helping a psychiatrist to understand the person, as they haven't had the privilege that I have had, in terms of meeting the person and all of the key people and the person's world.

Here, we can see how skills in understanding and traversing diverse paradigms in mental health can create advocacy opportunities within a multidisciplinary setting.

Working Towards Alternatives to Coercive Mental Health Responses

Through a critical approach to systemic work, we can also make changes so that we are not only limited to buffering the effects of the mental health system in people's lives once they are already interfacing with it (see Chaps. 3 and 4), but also providing alternative pathways for people, outside coercive interventions. We discussed the importance of this, since treatment in the mental health system can be very harmful, particularly in the context of involuntary interventions, frequently amplifying distress (Daley et al., 2019; Daya, 2022), and the mental health system is often limited to offering coercive interventions at times of crisis (Whitaker et al., 2021). Our analysis in Chaps. 3 and 4 explored what happens when social workers bring a social justice perspective to the mental health field and the complexities of navigating oppressive mental health system contexts. However, our work does not need to end here. Through systemic advocacy, we can move beyond bolstering the existing system, and work towards supporting people to access alternative forms of care and resources so less harm is done. As noted by Barbie:

> In the systemic work that I do is it's actually about keeping people out of the public mental health system. There's two ways of keeping people out of the system. I'm not talking about gatekeeping and keeping people out of services if they actually want to enter the system, through denying support. I'm thinking more about how I actually don't think that public mental health services are particularly advantageous for people to be engaged in for a whole range of reasons. The complete control and paternalism and the idea 'we actually know what's better for you'. And so, I believe as social workers it's part of our role to equip people with the knowledge that there are alternatives, because I actually think the state-based mental health system is dangerous for everybody, including workers and clients.

In this way, we can expand our understandings of mental health social work so that we are not merely adopting the perspective of our organisation, but rather, drawing on knowledges regarding mental health system harms, and the importance of addressing the social contexts of distress. For example, Barbie spoke about setting up a group for young women who had experienced sexual assault, and who were currently receiving mental health services. The opportunity to meet together provided a sharp contrast to their experience within a diagnostic-focused mental health setting:

> So that they could recognise the commonality of their experiences, but also to know each other. There were huge barriers that we had to overcome for the group to be allowed, because of the so-called 'risk'. It was so advantageous for those young women to come together, and when it did happen, it was, of course, very successful.

Finding and arguing for alternative options, beyond a mainstream mental health service response, requires creative and thoughtful approaches which demonstrate humility about the limitations of professional knowledges and an imagination about a world beyond traditional human services.

Adopting a Collective Approach

Our research revealed how multidisciplinary teamwork, systemic advocacy, and cultural change work cannot be done effectively as a 'lone' social worker but needs to happen in connection with a supportive community of critical workers and through relationship building across an organisation and sector more broadly, including building strong connections with people with lived experience. Otherwise, pushing for change can quickly become unsustainable or misguided. Indeed, our cooperative inquiry research process, in which we met together to discuss critical perspectives on mental health, provided opportunities for solidarity, peer support, and countering isolation (see Chap. 6 for a more detailed discussion). Barbie identified the need to:

> Find powerful allies and combine our energies. It might be your allies are powerful, because there are emotionally powerful and they sustain you. Other allies might have structural power. They have the stroke of the pen, and they can fund things or they can approve things.

Such diverse relationships have the potential to support social workers in navigating and locating points of resistance in the complex terrain of mental health social work, and even more importantly, to remain accountable in practice.

Building Relationships and Understanding Systems

Our reflective conversations revealed that opening up possibilities for systems change often involves building working relationships with people on multidisciplinary teams who have differing views and priorities (as initially discussed in Chap. 4). In this way, advocacy work not only involves 'taking a stand' in medicalised workplaces against the limitations of biomedical neoliberalism but also involves highly relational and strategic work in challenging the status quo within interdisciplinary contexts. As discussed by Cassidy:

> It's about understanding the priorities of management or different departments, and then trying to work within those priorities to state your case. In community work, organisations can become quite concerned with mitigating risk, which often translates into more processes, more gathering of data, for example, requiring registration information from people to access groups or to access events and then categorising people. There's a concern towards reputational and litigation-related risk, which can overshadow the value of community work. Social workers can play a role in trying to mitigate a risk orientation. They can advocate to make policies more open and flexible, and reduce the amount of information required from participants, at least at first. So, for example, people can come and enter a community space, and do a registration form later. Advocacy is a skill that can be learned and practiced.

This example illustrates a possibility within social work practice for promoting accessibility to non-medicalised community resources, and challenging taken-for-granted assumptions and priorities set by management. This is enacted by firstly understanding the existing systems and agendas, and then working strategically within the constraints of an organisation's requirements to develop an alternative approach.

Working Strategically and Relationally Across Difference

Focusing on division among two binary positions can focus our attention on defining differences, lessening the possibilities for change and rendering social workers less responsible for enacting change, because we are able to blame those who disagree with us (Fook, 2016). In contrast to this approach, Beatrice provided the reflection:

> The team is also a community, and until you establish relationships with people, you can't start challenging them—because you need to understand their perspective in order to be effective. It doesn't mean you have to agree or fit in with them, but what it does mean is that you've got a basis to advocate from.

Importantly, in this example, the goal was not conflict avoidance, or agreement among all, nor to eliminate discomfort as a result of different perspectives, as this is part of the experience of challenging the status quo. We reflected on how, within highly fraught and complex contexts, effective multidisciplinary teamwork takes time and commitment. It is imperfect, ongoing, and contested. While social work is well-attuned to the relational aspects of our face-to-face work with people and communities, it is possible that the relational and strategic aspects of social work advocacy in multidisciplinary contexts are sometimes understated (Fook, 2016). This is understandable, given the crisis-oriented nature of many of our workplaces, and the ethical orientation that many social workers hold towards enacting social justice; it makes sense that we want to enact change as quickly as possible. However, to hold colleagues accountable, we need to have existing relationships of respect and dignity (Reynolds, 2019). In an outcome-orientated approach to advocacy, which focuses on specific events in time, it is possible we may become overly reactive and miss out on a more integrated, relational, long-term, and iterative approach to advocacy, including opportunities for:

> interwoven levels, paths, directions, and moments that weave in and out of the present moment, the past and the future simultaneously, leaving us with multiple opportunities for creating and harnessing social and interpersonal power (Wahab et al., 2022, p. 152).

Through a process-driven and relational approach, we can start to make space to disrupt the idea that there is 'one' biomedical pathway to support wellbeing, and to question taken-for-granted assumptions, as noted by Margaret: *'All that focus then is on risk and fear. Where is the space for opportunities or potential? We don't get to talk about that at all'*. This approach differs from an episodic approach to advocacy, as it is not only about responding to discrete events as they occur, but working towards a broader paradigm shift within an organisation or team. As described by Barbie, organisational change involves persistence, a commitment to elevating lived experience knowledges, understanding systems, and working strategically:

> It's about always having your eye on the prize—to improve services and better outcomes; tenacity and being really strategic; problem-solving and negotiation; really understanding how the system works and how to work around it; working with the system, so actually using the energy of the system, to manoeuvre your way through. Not fighting the system face on but actually ducking and weaving. Making sure that your work is really driven by what people with lived experience are saying is important and what's needed.

Such approaches require putting in the time to build relationships, developing a deep understanding of the systems we are working in without becoming inducted into them, explaining why we are arguing for a socio-political rather than biomedical or neoliberal approach, and demonstrating confidence and knowledge in naming the benefits of a paradigm shift. Building trusted connections with critical colleagues who can keep us accountable in this work is a crucial strategy to ensure that we sustain our resistance, do not become aligned to the mainstream organisational agenda, and maintain an ethical stance of social justice.

Interrogating Our Own Assumptions and Practices

In addition to negotiating perspectives on a multidisciplinary team, we also discussed the significance of an ongoing interrogation of our own practice and assumptions. As Sarah noted, *there is a fine line between transformation and complicity*. Throughout this book, we have explored how social work's value base espouses a social justice stance, but social workers are not separate from psychiatric oppression and social work is implicated in mental health system harms. We should not assume a position of innocence in the work, nor can we rely on simply using more emancipatory language or making performative changes within organisations, in the absence of more transformative shifts away from coercion and control. As Sarah said:

> There is a clear preoccupation within mental health services regarding 'changing the language'—as though that's going to transform the system. What's missing, when people talk about recovery-oriented language, is a deep-seated reluctance to talk about violence. There is violence in people's lives when they enter the mental health system, but the ways in which the mental health system then enacts further violence on people's lives is often not talked about. Such experiences include sexual assault and harassment on the inpatient wards, all of the gendered diagnoses that are assigned to women and the ways in which the violence in their life is concealed, in addition to the use of psychotropic medications to control and contain women's emotions and responses to violence.

Indeed, it is concerning to see more and more human service organisations claiming to be 'trauma-informed', when there often remains a significant gap between such claims and the realities of receiving a service (Brown, 2024). We discussed the need for social work to remain vigilant to the tokenistic ways in which language can be used by organisations to provide a veneer of meaningful change, while continuing status quo practices.

Listening to Ethical Pain and Leaving an Oppressive Workplace

Having described the possibilities for advocacy and systems change, we do not want to portray an overly idealistic vision of multidisciplinary teamwork and culture change. Many of us have left workplaces, where it was not possible to find spaces to successfully challenge oppressive practices. Moral injury is a well-documented aspect of mental health work, given the disconnections between coercive practices and social justice values (Suslovic, 2024). In these circumstances, social workers may make decisions to place their time and resources elsewhere, when vested interests and entrenched coercive and oppressive practices prove impenetrable. As discussed by Scarlett:

> You couldn't rock the boat, so that was why I resigned in the end—I was asked to stop raising my concerns. Management didn't want to rupture the relationships with the key stakeholders that were funding our service. I think the moral distress started when I recognised the harm that was occurring when systems were failing children and then you're asked by managers to stop noticing that and stop advocating for something different. I could no longer be complicit in a system where I and the stakeholders around me could not guarantee even the physical safety of children, let alone their emotional wellbeing in residential care.

Here, the ethical pain that social workers experience in oppressive organisational contexts was positioned as meaningful information, extending far beyond simplistic and pathologising notions of worker 'burnout' (Reynolds, 2012). An analysis of contexts, power relations, and the politics of experience can help social workers to make meaning of their reactions within systems that do not reflect their personal and professional values. This example demonstrates that leaving an organisation can be part of an ongoing commitment to social justice and an ethical stance in relation to systemic harm.

Overall, the range and diversity within these examples demonstrate how resistance is not neat or clear-cut; rather, it is 'as an assemblage of practices that interact with restricting regimes of governance' (Strier & Bershtling, 2016, p.113). This demonstrates the value for ongoing learning, curiosity, collaboration, humility, and reflection. In the next chapter, we discuss the significance of the cooperative inquiry process in providing a space for us to experience such possibilities.

Concluding Reflections

The discussion in this chapter is not about elevating one form of work over another; as we have explored at length in Chaps. 3 and 4, a critical lens can be applied in 'clinical' work, to open possibilities for resisting the limitations of a managerialist and biomedical paradigm. However, beyond considering these opportunities, it is necessary to redress an imbalance in contemporary social work understandings of mental health practice, which have become very narrowly attuned to individual-focused work, reflecting neoliberal values. There are opportunities across a range of contexts for social work to enact more community-based approaches, as is evident in Frankie's example of a regular barbeque, which was developed in the context of a service that is primarily focused on individual casework. In this way, an openness to a more collectivist orientation across all contexts of social work practice is useful in challenging an unhelpful binary between social workers who work with individuals and social workers who are located in community contexts. By drawing on creativity and collectivism into our work, locating 'personal' concerns within socio-political contexts, and thinking outside the norms of 'fixing individuals', we can consider ways to influence systemic changes in our workplaces that recognise the inherently political nature of all our work. Through community building approaches, we can start to integrate practices that identify and respond to systems of harm, rather than reproducing deficit-focused practices, although it is important to remain humble and reflexive about our own positioning as employees within oppressive workplaces (Fook, 2016). In addition, our discussions explored the buzzwords of 'co-design' and 'collaboration' (McKercher, 2020), which opened up opportunities to interrogate what is needed to develop meaningful relationships of solidarity, avoiding the hazards of rushing in, being an expert, and engaging in tokenism. Beyond this reflexivity, it is crucial to acknowledge the myriad forms of peer-led community building have emerged outside the scope of services altogether (the Hearing Voices Network, Soteria House, Wildflower Alliance, and Alternatives to Suicide, to name a few). There is much for social work to learn from the activism of people and communities with lived experience, who have said 'enough is enough' in response to system harms and created generative, alternative approaches outside the constraints of the mental health system (Davidow & Mazel-Carlton, 2020).

Through an analysis of power, we can be vigilant regarding the need to 'look upstream' (Karban, 2017) and over time, develop an ability to clearly articulate the intrinsic connections between social inequalities, violence, and distress. A key social work skill is an ability to communicate such connections, and to articulate the value of approaches extending beyond an individual-diagnostic paradigm, to diverse audiences who may be attached to a traditional medicalised perspective, while also remaining learners and being keenly attuned to radical alternatives emerging beyond the scope of professionalised service provision. Through considering the possibilities for a meaningful paradigm shift in mental health, we can move beyond social work practice that is solely focused on buffering the effects of oppressive systems on people's lives, towards a more transformative agenda of social change (Whitaker et al., 2021). Such advocacy needs to be enacted with humility, so that we are not overstating our role or ignoring the paradoxes of our location within oppressive systems, as we explored in Chap. 2. Through working collaboratively with groups and communities, in ways that challenge risk-oriented and diagnostic discourses, possibilities can emerge to disrupt the limitations of a crisis-driven and pathologising mental health system.

References

Brown, C. (2021). Critical clinical social work and the neoliberal constraints on social justice in mental health. *Research on Social Work Practice, 31*(6), 644–652.

Brown, C. (2024). Reframing trauma through social justice: Resisting the politics of mainstream trauma discourse. Taylor & Francis.

Carey, M., & Foster, V. (2011). Introducing 'deviant' social work: Contextualising the limits of radical social work whilst understanding (fragmented) resistance within the social work labour process. *British Journal of Social Work, 41*(3), 576–593.

Clarke, J., & Morley, C. (2022). Risk assessments and critical social work. In J. Maidment, R. Egan, R. Tudor, & S. Nipperess (Eds.), *Practice skills in social work and welfare* (pp. 141–154). Routledge.

Cohen, S. (1998). *Against criminology*. Routledge.

Chapman, A., Williams, C., Hannah, J., & Pūras, D. (2020). Reimagining the mental health paradigm for our collective Well-being. *Health and Human Rights, 22*(1), 1.

Daley, A., Costa, L., & Beresford, P. (2019). *Madness, violence, and power: A critical collection*. University of Toronto Press.

Davidow, S., & Mazel-Carlton, C. (2020). The "alternatives to suicide" approach: A decade of lessons learnt. In A. Page & W. Stritzke (Eds.), *Alternatives to suicide: Beyond risk and toward a life worth living* (pp. 179–199). Academic Press.

Daya, I. (2022). Russian dolls and epistemic crypts: A lived experience reflection on epistemic injustice and psychiatric confinement. *Incarceration, 3*(2).

Egan, M., Friedman, V. J., Jones, D. R., Rhew, N. D., Robinson, S., & Sama, L. M. (2024). *Restorative action research: Fostering wellbeing as a collective, relational, vital endeavor*. Action Research.

Howard, A., & Rawsthorne, M. (2020). *Everyday community practice: Principles and practice*. Routledge.

Finley, L., Esposito, L., & Hall, L. (2012). Neoliberalism and the non-profit industrial complex: The limits of a market approach to service delivery. *Peace Studies Journal, 5*(3), 4-26.

Fook, J. (2016). *Social work: A critical approach to practice*. Sage.

Gasdaglis, K. (2025). Whose anger matters? Methodological mistakes in the philosophy of emotion. *Feminist Philosophy Quarterly, 11*(1).

Josewski, V., de Leeuw, S., & Greenwood, M. (2023). Grounding wellness: Coloniality, placeism, land, and a critique of "social" determinants of indigenous mental health in the Canadian context. *International Journal of Environmental Research and Public Health, 20*(5), 4319.

Karban, K. (2017). Developing a health inequalities approach for mental health social work. *British Journal of Social Work, 47*(3), 885–992.

McKercher, K. (2020). *Beyond sticky notes: Codesign for real: Mindsets*. Methods & Movements.

Mehrotra, G. R. (2023). How we do the work is the work: Building an intersectional queer praxis for critical feminist scholarship. *Affilia, 38*(4), 555–569.

Medina, J. (2013). *The epistemology of resistance: Gender and racial oppression, epistemic injustice, and the social imagination*. Oxford University Press.

Muller, K. (2005). Journeys of freedoms: responding to the effects of domestic violence. *International Journal of Narrative Therapy & Community Work, 2005*(3/4), 106–118.

O'leary, P., Tsui, M. S., & Ruch, G. (2013). The boundaries of the social work relationship revisited: Towards a connected, inclusive and dynamic conceptualisation. *British Journal of Social Work, 43*(1), 135–153.

Papadopoulos, A., & Maylea, C. (2020). Medicare funded mental health social work: Better access to what? *Australian Social Work, 73*(2), 137–148.

Parker, I. (2017). Marxist theory and psychotherapy. In B. Cohen (Ed.), *Routledge international handbook of critical mental health* (pp. 244–250). Routledge.

Pease, B. (2020). From evidence-based practice to critical knowledge in post-positivist social work. In B. Pease, J. Allan, & L. Briskman (Eds.), *Critical social work* (pp. 45–57). Routledge.

Reynolds, V. (2012). An ethical stance for justice-doing in community work and therapy. *Journal of Systemic Therapies, 31*(4), 18–33.
Reynolds, V. (2019). The zone of fabulousness. *Context, 164*, 36–39.
Salter, L. (2021). Research as an act of resistance: Responsive, temporally framed narrative inquiry. *International Review of Qualitative Research, 14*(3), 383–397.
Sinclair, A., Mahboub, L., Gillieatt, S., & Fernandes, C. (2023). 'You just treat me like a human being': Using lived experience to (re) imagine boundary practices in mental health settings. *The British Journal of Social Work, 53*(3), 1408–1425.
Strier, R., & Bershtling, O. (2016). Professional resistance in social work: Counterpractice assemblages. *Social Work, 61*(2), 111–118.
Suslovic, B. (2024). Abolition of involuntary mental health services. In C. Franklin (Ed.), *Encyclopedia of social work*. Oxford University Press.
Tseris, E., Franks, S. & Hart, E.B. (2024). Psychiatric oppression in women's lives. Palgrave.
Wahab, S., Mehrotra, G. R., & Myers, K. E. (2022). Slow scholarship for social work: A praxis of resistance and creativity. *Qualitative Social Work, 21*(1), 147–159.
Watts, L., & Hodgson, D. (2019). *Social justice theory and practice for social work*. Springer.
Whitaker, L., Smith, F. L., Brasier, C., Petrakis, M., & Brophy, L. (2021). Engaging with transformative paradigms in mental health. *International Journal of Environmental Research and Public Health, 18*(18), 9504.

Chapter 6
Holding the Fine Line Between Transformation and Complicity

Our conversations in this practice research project confirmed that mental health social work continues to seek to progress social justice, and as a collective we believed *change is possible* (Sarah). Moving beyond an articulation of how existing power arrangements in the mental health system entrench inequality and oppression, the social work practices discussed in the previous chapters of this book aimed to foster social justice in ways that are aligned with the values and ethics of the profession. By calling for alternative ways of talking about children's situations, Scarlett promotes a *culture where it is not ok to unnecessarily pathologise children and young people in team discussions*. As Alyssa's *clinical work is based around changing systems*, she actively *reframes the narrative around mental health and wellbeing to one that focuses on the person and not the Western way of looking at mental health and wellbeing, which is trying to fit you back into a capitalist functioning nine-to-five world*. Instead, she *builds up internal protective factors like connection to culture and Country*. Iris sees *those extra aspects to the person's world, for example, violence, trauma, poverty and brings that into the formulation and into the perspective of the team*. Cassidy *always looks towards challenging the biomedical model, finding opportunities, even within clinical positions, to destabilise or affect power relations*. Fundamentally, as Alyssa said, we *do not take the status quo as the status quo*. Thus, we have taken on board the brief of the profession and through resistant imagining (Medina, 2013) have worked towards both small and larger ways of fostering systems enabling wellbeing. Such resistance does not necessarily make for comfortable work experiences. As Iris said, *while social justice is what I got into mental health social work for, it's what made the work uncomfortable … but it's also why I stayed*.

To set the scene for investigating social work's navigation of the paradoxes emerging from working within systems it seeks to transform, in Chap. 2, we explored how these paradoxes emerge. Recognising the ongoing impact of colonisation while being descendants of colonisers or those colonised, we seek to not only resist colonialism but to de-colonise mental health care. Acknowledging our

L. Whitaker et al., *Social Work in the Mental Health Field*, SpringerBriefs in Social Work, https://doi.org/10.1007/978-3-032-08306-7_6

complicity with entrenched global capitalism, we seek to recognise the brokenness of systems as well as the beauty of survivorship and the non-human world beyond economic value. Admitting to engaging in biomedical discourse when seeking recognition alongside other mental health professionals, we adopt accessible, inclusive language to stand with those with lived experience of distress. Accepting fears of legal consequences for misjudging risk, we advocate for human rights to prevail. In short, by recognising how the political infiltrates the lives of people experiencing distress and those practising social work, we can at least not settle for simple dichotomous positioning or the perpetuation of systemic oppression. Instead, we can grasp opportunities to envisage and enact a transformed paradigm.

We explored social work practices for fostering social justice when working with individuals, groups, and communities when navigating these paradoxes and acknowledged these practices called for *leaning into the complexity of people's lives and not knowing* (Sarah). In Chap. 3, we identified relational social work practices honouring the complexity of people's lives and centring lived experience while exposing the influences of socio-political contexts. In Chap. 4, we questioned concepts of 'person-centred', 'recovery-oriented', 'trauma-informed' approaches and 'risk', acknowledging the role of advocacy in social work practice. In Chap. 5, we expanded our gaze to working in solidarity with communities, naming the tensions that emerge when introducing a community-oriented approach given the domination of managerialism in mental health services. We discussed strategies for managing competing agendas, highlighting *the fine line between transformation and complicity* (Sarah). In brief, we acknowledged the complexities of *getting work done while addressing power* (Frankie); consistently thinking about *how those things happen together* (Frankie).

In this chapter, we explore how we have positioned ourselves to nurture capacity and capability for holding a transformative line. The career stories we share reveal a search for spaces and places supporting, indeed championing, creative approaches to social justice in this field, while also highlighting ethical tensions. We begin by examining the choices we have made in our careers in aiming towards enacting a power analysis in practice.

Nurturing Social Work Practice Cultivating Social Justice in Mental Health

While our career paths vary, they have been underpinned by a commitment to social work's brief for social justice in mental health. As social work students, we came to mental health social work practice with a passion for justice. Cassidy, for example, *wanted to do social work to change systems to be more fair and more centred on the people who rely on those systems to survive*. Those of us in academic positions, like Sarah, have been *amazed by students' openness, passion, and enthusiasm. It is almost like questions about human rights are not being asked, and as soon as you provide an invitation, people want this*. However, transitioning from university into the mental health service sector is challenging. Iris captured the experience of many of us when she described initially trying *to adapt and learn about the medical model and diagnosis and medication.* This adaptation left Iris *really uncomfortable and really unsettled.... It wasn't what [she] was passionate about, or what [she] had learnt at university or why [she] came to the work. It wasn't any of those things*. We witnessed *the harms that were happening* (Margaret) while developing mental health 'literacy', and we could not believe that we had not been prepared for how exhausting the work might be. Perhaps it was inevitable that we would become *disheartened by social work and the directions it has taken in the mental health space* (Scarlett). However, there were turning points. Iris, for example, realised:

> The things that make social work in mental health practice hard, are the same reasons why we should be there. It is difficult for us, because the model of care is sometimes so different to social work. But that's why we should be there, because we can bring that perspective of the social and political contexts of people's lives to the forefront.

Seeking to claim the social justice brief that inspired us, we moved into work roles we hoped would enable greater influence towards systemic and social change. Our career decisions were prompted by an interest in a cohort, such as women, and/or a view regarding the possibilities within particular contexts—for example, non-government organisations that espoused a practice framework aligned with values of social justice. We sought to work with colleagues with a reputation for *doing advocacy and meaningful systems change* (Frankie). Barbie positioned herself in strategic social policy work after she imagined system change as *like breaking a globe with a hammer and chisel. You can knock it on the outside, and it will fracture. But if you're further in, you can knock out more*. At the same time, the challenges of working 'inside' the system can be enormous, and Scarlett discussed how important it is to be attuned to ethical pain and to know when to leave a workplace that is perpetrating harm. Beatrice chose to move into program management because *good management and funding mobilised change*, whereas Alyssa took on the role of supervisor to *encourage other people to have a reflective practice approach on what they're doing and to be able to change systems*. Some career choices might have been expedient, for better pay to finance our lives and families, demonstrating social work's paradoxical embeddedness in capitalist arrangements, rather than a 'neat' social justice narrative. Other changes in workplace occurred when it was no longer *ethical to stay around; when I didn't have the energy to give the people the absolute best service* (Frankie).

Whether serendipitous, expedient, or strategically planned, we recognised *moving between the layers from the grassroots to the systems, and maybe back again* (Sarah) could be a helpful strategy in contributing to social change. As Alyssa straddles *direct client work and the supervision work*, she is *able to advocate for systems change* on the basis of regular contact with people experiencing distress as well as social workers who are working in systems. Similarly, after moving into a policy position, Frankie has *specifically been able to leverage 'clinical' and frontline experience to influence policy*. She had originally envisaged policy work as *a compromise to frontline work where [she]could do the most ethical work, where [she] could make the most change, where [she]could be the most supportive of people in community*. Her views shifted. However, she noted that she will probably return to a direct practice or community-oriented role in the future. She now concurs with Barbie that:

> Your skill is where you get the most joy and where you feel that you make the most impact. That's what gives me joy… It doesn't matter whether you're outside or inside the system. Critical perspectives need to be everywhere in the mental health field.

As social justice informs practice wherever we work, the question is *Where am I most useful?* (Frankie). We are sustained by securing positions where our *set of skills brings the greatest influence* (Barbie). At the same time, our research identified the ongoing challenge of resisting invitations to become socialised into the systems we aim to transform, leading to the hazards of engaging in surface-level reform efforts that do not adequately challenge coercive and biomedical practices (Roper et al., 2023). Ongoing accountability practices, dialogue across contexts, and critical reflection on the difference between understanding systems and becoming inducted into systems are therefore crucial. We look for bosses who are going to *let you fly rather than bring you down* (Barbie). We seek to call lateral violence for what it is. We sought variety in the work by working across part-time positions because *you can't advocate five days a week* (Alyssa). Continual learning from global wisdom informing social change involves *questioning: Who am I reading? Whose voices are more prominent? And whose not?* (Frankie). This attention to what is happening outside the dominant paradigm—keeping up to date with critical mental health and Mad Studies scholarship, for example—is particularly important so that we do not become blinkered by the system. For Cassidy, possibilities can be opened up by *joining or starting committees and working groups* to start different, more politicised conversations about 'mental health'. By seeking out allies and working collectively, and in solidarity with people with direct experiences of mental health system harm, as Barbie said, avoids being *sucked into being the innovative hero… The innovative hero will fall over eventually, because one of us alone cannot make the change*. Working together, we may get beyond *imagining… limited by the constructions that we've been given… that are limited by the culture… You've got to be able to verbalise it and refine it, and then see if it works with others, because it is a collective resistance* (Barbie). As Alyssa says, *individuals don't have the power to change systems, collectives have the power to change systems*.

Career Stories

Here we recount stories of our experience of cultivating social justice through our social work practice in the mental health field.

'Creating a Better System' (Alyssa)

Mental health social work is not something I fell into. I made that choice after having my own lived experience of accessing mental health systems. The reason I'm in the mental health profession is because I had a poor experience of using mental health systems. It was traumatic to say the very least. It was not good enough and I went back to university to do my social work degree. This lived experience informs how I do my work. I ensure there are therapeutic services for Aboriginal people that are culturally appropriate. I genuinely don't know how I ended up in a management role but all the roles I've taken on are with the intention of creating a better system that does not rely on the medical model.

Having a power perspective means you do not take the status quo as the status quo. You're inherently asking questions about: Why are we doing this? What is the meaning behind this? What is the purpose behind this? Therefore, you are not just following a care plan or following a wellbeing plan because you're being told to. You're not perpetuating that cycle of just doing things because we've always done them.

All the roles I do are based around changing systems. In my current role, I am building a new system for Aboriginal mental health within the District. In my other role as a supervisor, I encourage other people to have a reflective practice approach on what they're doing and to be able to change systems. All my roles, apart from direct therapeutic work, are ones that encourage people to either look at the system or change the system.

I can't advocate 5 days a week sustainably. After working full time for about 2 years and becoming burnt out, I realised that was not a sustainable way for me in this field and I switched to part time. Doing direct client work and the supervision work extends the reach of being able to advocate for systems change. Also, I couldn't work in a hospital full time. It's too much. It would have burnt me out. It's more sustainable to work part time and be in the field for decades, rather than in the field for a couple of years.

'Bringing a Macro Awareness Within Our Micro Practice' (Scarlett)

A power analysis and a commitment to social justice shaped the decisions I made throughout my career in mental health. Over the years, though, I found unhelpful binary ways of thinking about power in this field, that is, working towards social change can only occur in policy or system reform and not in individual work per se. In my first social work placement in Community Adult Mental Health, I was really focused on macro structures that create enduring and unequal power relationships in people's lives and the need for structural change. My supervisor was very generous in inviting me to consider how this macro power analysis could inform how I work individually with people in micro interactions. I initially worked in non-government organisations because I wanted to work in organisations with an explicit socially just practice framework. For example, I really enjoyed working in a feminist organisation which encouraged an astute power analysis in both individual therapy work and social action work to recognise the oppressive gendered nature of sexual violence against young women, and how distress for women occurs in a patriarchal society.

When I commenced working at a tertiary mental health service for children and young people, I felt so uncomfortable about participating in diagnosis and formulation, because I felt like it was overlooking the macro context of children's lives. A colleague reminded me that formulation is an opportunity to tell a story about what is occurring for the person. I wanted to find socio-political ways of naming children and young peoples' politics of experiences. I tried to find ways to navigate 'assessment', 'intervention', and stakeholder work processes to identify and respond to the oppressive structures in the child or young person's social contexts. At times, I was the only person at the table offering a different perspective, to widen the focus, and avoid pathologising labels. While I could see the multidisciplinary team's way of talking about children and young people changing over time, the longer I stayed in this role, the more clearly I recognised the systemic harm being done to children in 'residential care' settings. I also realised I was not separate from this system. I was a part of it and complicit within it. When I was asked by management to stop writing advocacy letters, I knew I could no longer stay in the role.

Since doing my PhD, I have developed a heightened awareness about how power is everywhere, in every micro interaction we have as social workers. In my research, I am committed to making visible the contradictions in the field and how social workers navigate these tensions. I feel like social work as a profession is at a crossroads. With the increasing dominance of psychological discourses, we are invited to 'skill-up' in the latest evidence-based individual therapy interventions, which overlooks the macro intersecting forms of oppression. I think we have a real opportunity to continue to articulate and critically reflect on how a macro power analysis informs our micro practice with individuals and communities.

'Changing Systems to Be More Fair and More Centred on the People Who Rely on Those Systems to Survive' (Cassidy)

I wanted to do social work, to change systems to be more fair and more centred on the people who rely on those systems to survive. For me, advocacy and having an understanding of power has been really important in choosing the kind of work that I do. Sometimes that has meant doing roles that are broader than some traditional social work roles, or at least broadening the role that I am in, to suit me and my priorities in the work. Even if I am working within a position description that's quite limited, I always look for ways to expand that, in a way that is challenging the biomedical model—finding opportunities, even within clinical positions, to destabilise or affect power relations. So, in a lot of roles that I have done, I have joined or started committees and working groups. That has involved a lot of relational work with the other staff in the organisation and bringing them along for the journey of looking at the service and saying: How can we make this better practice? How can we improve this service for the people who use it? Sometimes there is resistance, if there is quite a structured hierarchy or taken-for-granted ways of working. I've found that it's important to learn to use your voice, in a way that's really pragmatic. I do my best to find allies, and adopting a community care rather than self-care approach. That's sometimes within the workspace and sometimes outside of the workspace. And I always try to bring my leaders along for the ride as well, and use the language of the organisation to make it appealing for leaders to adopt a more critical approach, or at least allow me to. With the increased bureaucratisation of social work, there are all the different categories of social workers. I worry about that categorisation and the hierarchy that it creates within social work itself. It does not do the work of destabilising power relations at all. It means that social work becomes a version of psychology, really. I would like to see some appreciation for what got me into social work, how broad social work is, and how we can use our skills in a dynamic and diverse variety of ways.

'Where Am I Most Useful?' (Frankie)

An analysis of power has influenced what I do massively. It has influenced the decisions I've made about where I work. I remember a lecture at uni when someone was talking about being 'in the tent' (trying to make changes within a mainstream setting) or being 'outside the tent'. I think about that a lot. Where am I most useful?

An analysis of power informs my practice, how I work, and how I engage with other people—trying to take a more collaborative approach to the work. It has to be an active choice every single day, with every decision that you make, with the intention of going into the work and knowing that there's going to be pushback. I think that's the ethical imperative that we have coming into the space with a critical lens, recognising that it's tiring—it's easier just to pump out a task. It's a paradox because you also want to build relationships and they can be hard to build if colleagues feel like you're agitating.

I see other social workers, and I feel like they're kind of just gliding through. And I'm constantly grappling with these ideas—the balance of getting work done and also addressing power. How do those things happen together? We're doing the best we can in the environment. And is that good enough? Can I enact change in the ways that I want to? Am I able analyse power and use my skill-set and use a critical social work framework in this environment?

What we're talking about is addressing injustice in people's lives—that's mental health social work; addressing the injustices that people have experienced, either interpersonally or via our systems.

I feel like to be ethical, there needs to be an element of self-reflection around how your own life could take a turn at any minute—especially when you hear the stories of women protecting their children. I think that can be a really powerful lens to work through.

Continual learning has been really important. Who am I reading? Whose voices are more prominent? When I'm seeking training, trying to analyse and critique where that training has come from, whose voices are prioritised. I think a critical perspective is found in the continual noticing; it's in clinical supervision. I've tried to start writing now as well, and it's in the reading. So for me, it's staying in touch with all of those ways. And being in conversation and in community with others, so that my peers can hold me accountable.

'Don't Get Sucked in by the System: What We Bring to the System is a Critical Lens' (Barbie)

A long time ago… I sat on a hill somewhere, and thought about what's the point of greatest impact in mental health services? I thought about the globe, about this ball, and a hammer and chisel. You can knock the globe on the outside and it will fracture. But if you're inside the globe you can get greater bang for your buck. But which part do you go into?

It took a long time for that to come to fruition but [inside the system is] definitely where I am now, as I'm working in the government in a social policy role. I'm working where the decisions are made about the care that people get inside the system. The tension is, in taking such opportunities to drive change, do we prop up a broken system?

There's so much work to be done. It doesn't actually matter where you pitch, everywhere is as important. Your skill is where you get the most joy and where you feel that you make the most impact. You know, you can do reform, you can do revolution. It doesn't matter whether you're outside or inside the system. Critical perspectives need to be everywhere in the mental health field. For me, it's the point of greatest influence. So, my critical perspective on power is, I look at where my set of skills brings me to the greatest point of influence, because that's where the greatest concentration of power is.

In terms of positioning myself in my career, I look for who my boss is going to be. You want people who'll lift you up with them, not take you down because they bought into patriarchal notions. In health settings, there is something about patriarchy, teaching women to be competitive with each other. There's an extraordinary amount of lateral violence.

The other thing you look for is allies. Always there are allies in every part of the system. So, you find your allies, whether you're in decision-making positions, whether you're in therapeutic positions, whether you're in academic positions. So, you find your allies. That's collective power. We have to have a collective vision.

'Chipping Away at Dominant Ways of Thinking Within the System' (Margaret)

When I first graduated, I wanted to be in a non-government organisation (NGO) because I had this idea that I would never work for the government. I thought government systems are inherently methods of controlling the population, so I wanted to stay outside of that as much as possible. So I worked for NGO organisations where there was a clearly defined social justice position, where their organisational vision aligned with the kind of work that I wanted to do, having more of a sense of agency, and freedom [in my practice]. But then I moved to the UK, and it's just a different system. There are not many NGOs. So when I came back to Australia, I joined a mental health service for children and young people. I started working out my perspective on power. I was thinking about diagnosis and being able to advocate with people both internal to the organisation and external to the organisation, so that the kind of formulation I provided was more important than the diagnosis, or that their diagnosis could be kind of matched to the experience of the person, to really help tell their story.

In working in the systems involved with the children and young people, I realised that it's such a compromised position that it's really hard to actually call people to account. It is ridiculous that certain stakeholders are not bringing the child to appointments, whereas I think when you're involved, you are trying to have this kind of understanding of the potential barriers [for the stakeholders]. I think then there's potential to accept substandard care, essentially, to maintain relationships [with stakeholders].

In my current team, the dominance of the medical model is really challenging. Bringing a power analysis has involved chipping away at dominant ways of thinking, and even the way we talk about children and young people. It takes a lot of time and energy. But we need to have people who can resist those dominant ways within the system.

I have wanted to elevate lived experience [in my team], as it fits so nicely with social work. I have intentionally partnered with the peer support worker as I do not want this work to be done in isolation, but to find a way to find space for this lived experience and for that knowledge and expertise to be shared with the team and others.

Social work is a big workforce in mental health. I'm thinking about opportunities to have a collective social work voice, and to explore what critical social work involves, to have a combination of some external voices, but also using the experience in the room in a much more of a meaningful way to start to engender a different dialogue in existing social work forums. I like the idea of being able to provide that helicopter view because of how easy it is to get inducted into systems, being able to offer a different perspective, or be able to help other social workers articulate a different perspective.

'Re-Imagining Mental Health Social Work and Resisting Complacency' (Sarah)

Attention to power and the politics of mental health has informed the priorities that I have now, because there's a lot of focus on particular experiences of distress that are often coming from people with privilege—these perspectives are valid and helpful in some ways, but we're not hearing from people who have experienced the most significant harms in the system. This silencing perpetuates the idea that the system is OK as it currently stands or only needs minor reforms or more funding. In contrast, I want to ask some deeper questions about what we're not talking about when we talk about mental health. We are talking more and more about mental health within contemporary Western contexts, but what are we not talking about? What other words could we use? What other things could we bring into the picture—colonialism, poverty, racism, and gendered violence to name a few? I am passionate about inviting some different questions and trying to re-imagine the space, rather than the persistent focus on fixing people and social control! Engaging with the survivor movement has been pivotal in developing my understandings of the actions being enacted across diverse contexts—truly disruptive ideas that extend beyond social work, and beyond current systems and institutions.

As a researcher, there can be a perceived separation from practice, as though we're no longer involved or complicit in psychiatric harm when we are located in university settings, but of course we are. The majority of funding is predicated on a biomedical framing of mental health, and we can be highly constrained in how we can do research, and even the questions that we can ask. So, I don't think social work is ever separate from these questions about power in the mental health field, regardless of our workplace context. Therefore, wherever I am located, it's about aiming to use the resources of the institution to open up the paradigm.

There are many times when I have felt extremely disheartened by social work—the biomedical directions that social work is taking in the mental health space, which has led to a sense of not belonging. Sometimes I have just wanted to run away from mental health social work, when it is conceptualised in a clinical way. But a more helpful approach has been to re-define it, or to contribute to re-defining it, and to reclaim a political analysis and actions. There are reasons to think that change is possible.

'It's What Makes the Work Uncomfortable and It's Also Why I Stayed' (Iris)

The things that make social work in mental health practice hard are the reasons why we should be there. We should be in this field because it is difficult for us, because at times it sits against our professional values. It can make you think: Can I be effective here? We should be there because we can bring that perspective of the social and the political context of people's lives to the forefront.

I came to social work because I was driven by my own personal values and this included a strong value of social justice. When I began working in the mental health field, it was a bit disheartening. I thought, all of this stuff I've learned at Uni is not valued here and is not the focus of the mental health field. What I tried to do initially was to adapt to that environment; to try and learn all I could about the medical model, diagnosis, and medication. But that was really uncomfortable and really unsettling for me because it wasn't a what I was passionate about, or what I had learnt at Uni, or why I came to the work. It wasn't any of those things and it can get you down.

Now, I think that discomfort was actually really helpful, because that is how our clients feel at times when accessing services. I had to learn how to lean into that discomfort and use it in a way that was going to be helpful for the work that I was doing. It was really important to look at power, and how power showed up in the relationship with the client. Ignoring the power dynamics or pretending that it does not exist is not helpful. So, needing to acknowledge that there is a level of power there and then, using that in a way that can influence, I guess not only the clients' care, but also the service itself. I might not have the power to make a diagnosis. I might not have the power to prescribe the medication in a mental health setting and that might be a big part of the focus of care. But I do have power to influence my colleagues and the system.

What I mean by that is seeing all of those extra aspects to the person's world, for example, violence, trauma, poverty, all of the other factors that we're so skilled at looking for and identifying as social workers, and bringing that into the formulation, bringing that into the perspective of the team. And I think when you have good relationships—and I don't want to downplay that because I think the relationship skills required are quite complex in this setting—but when you have good relationships with your colleagues and the other members of the multidisciplinary team, you can use that power of influence so much more. I don't mean influence in the negative sense of the word. I think it's been important to acknowledge it, and to get comfortable with it, and to learn ways of using it that are going to be beneficial to the clients that we work with. This is why I got into mental health. It's what makes the work uncomfortable. And it's also why I stayed.

'Experiments with Power and Influence: Navigating Dialectics and Paradoxes' (Beatrice)

After graduating I worked in mental health in a long-term inpatient setting for about 10 years. During that time, I joined a small community team where we had amazing rapport, professional respect, and complex, difficult discussions about our work. It was the early 90 s and psychiatry still had a psychosocial bent. Social work was welcomed as having a valid and important role. Through those conversations with peers and their respect for, and interest in, inquiry, I found my niche. I was inspired and curious about the nature of the change we were striving for. I enrolled in an advanced practice social work master's degree, read widely and in weekly, on-campus, small group tutorials, explored Gandhi and French feminists. I got excited about postmodernism. Acknowledging power differentials as products of structures, I wanted to experience different social structures such as cooperatives, and took a position coordinating a Women's Health Centre and living in an intentional community. Lengthy meetings and endless shared decision-making that were supposed to share power also stifled momentum. Whereas, good management and funding mobilised change.

What have I discovered? The path to imagining and fostering social arrangements promoting wellbeing is not simple. Conversations with colleagues, reflexivity and pondering the ideas of social thinkers have helped me to imagine. They help me to notice what is both present and missing from practice. How can we build on what we have already learnt?

The Research Process—'*Suddenly You Weren't Alone Because You Had Other People's Perspective or Strength Behind You*' (Margaret)

The cooperative inquiry that inspired this book embodied a developmental process of change. While each of the co-researchers knew someone in the group, many new relationships were formed as we fostered a community of practice where we experienced the '*joy of coming together*' (Barbie), enabling us to '*feel a little lighter*' (Margaret) (Egan et al., 2024; Palmer et al., 2018). By listening to one another as we grappled with articulating the practice wisdom we had developed, we co-created a unique opportunity to collectively reflect on mental health social work practice and share how we held ourselves accountable. The process sits well with First Nations practices, through a non-hierarchical and dialogical approach to knowledge-building. As our collective view spanned different states in Australia, academia, and sites of practice, as well as generations and cultural backgrounds, we were '*lifting our heads higher*' (Barbie) than our own situation. The collective voice, captured in the intertwined narrative of this book, was inspired by a shared language of power and diverse interpretations of addressing inequity in practice (McKenzie-Mohr & Lafrance, 2017). As the process spanned more than 12 months, as might be expected, our lives continued. A baby was born. We changed jobs. Our input varied as we were called to meet other demands on our time. We are delighted we pulled it off. By documenting a constellation of practices, from a diversity of experiences in mental health social work practice, we know we're '*not alone because we have other people's perspective and strength behind us*' (Margaret). These are our experiences of the research.

Alyssa

I have a bugbear about evidence-based stuff because I question who is the evidence based on? Everyone's looking at different evidence base and none of the evidence bases have Aboriginal people in it. Creating an evidence base is really tricky. The cooperative inquiry process is an accessible way of doing research.

It's been helpful for me to know other people who are aligned with how I view the world of mental health. I know what I believe and I'm very steadfast in it. Sometimes you can become a bit bogged down in everyone else's voices and it can make you question yourself. So, it's been helpful to have a bunch of other people who are aligned with the same values. Yes, it's about having someone in your corner. It's not that I need someone to come in and say 'you're right'. It's just having more people in your corner to know what I'm doing is correct.

Margaret

When I first joined the group, after the sessions, I almost felt lighter in my body. It was having a shared language and just hearing other people's experiences in diverse contexts. It was familiar; familiar challenges, familiar practices, and familiar ways of understanding the situation. I'm actually the only social worker in my team and the predominance of the medical model compromises respectful language. It has been really important to connect with people with a shared language and shared framework. This was really helpful. I felt less lonely and less isolated. It made a big difference on many levels. The lightness was really noticeable. I could see possibilities in terms of changing workplace cultures. It was like having permission to think about doing things differently. I've internalised members of the group. In situations I would wonder what others would be thinking. Suddenly you are not alone because you had other people's perspectives or strength behind you. Some of the stories that people have shared have really stayed with me as examples of great practice. There's been some modelling, and it's extended my practice. In the workplace, it can be easy to lose connection to what binds social work as a force, the way that we understand things, or our frameworks, systemic thinking. Having that collaboration in the group is a way of keeping that alive. What I've gained is a sense of doing things together and having a community behind me. I think it's important because the patriarchal biomedical model is so dominant, particularly in my current workplace, and so it requires a community response to be able to change, resist, and subvert. There's just more strength in doing things together, rather than being that sole voice.

Scarlett

The cooperative inquiry process has been really helpful for me because I was questioning how I can position myself in the mental health field that is not too compromising. It's been delightful to reflect as a collective from different points of view. It has been an opportunity to identify how we can be complicit in oppressive practice, to sit with this un-comfortability and re-think past practice experiences. It has been confirming for me to collectively acknowledge the messiness of social work practice and how we're not separate from the challenging contradictions we face in the field. It's been so inspiring to hear different practitioners' everyday forms of resistance within the biomedical paradigm and to learn a more nuanced social work practice. I enjoyed how we explored how we have all tried to navigate the contradictions, to not to provide the answers, as I don't think there's any neat solution, but to unpack the messy realities. I feel like this is the beginning of the story.

Barbie

I'm surprised that we could pull it off! Its strength is in the collective and that there's no right or wrong. Everything that we say is valid. People may or may not agree with us, but it doesn't make it wrong.

Like Margaret's pot, the rupture, and the mending with beautiful gold, the pottery binds it together. What I've learned and gained is that this couldn't have happened without each one of us. It had to have each one of us in it. If one of us was out of it, or another person was in it, it would be something different, equally as beautiful, but different.

It's also passing on of knowledge, isn't it? In the queer community, we talk about the importance of intergenerational intersectionality.

There is the joy of coming together. It helps me lift my head higher. Like consciousness raising in community development, we are now linked across several states across academia and several sites of practice.

Cassidy

I've loved it. I would love to do this all the time. All the involvement I've had has been really inspiring to me, and so wonderful to speak to other people who have similar and dissimilar experiences. It's been very useful to hear about everyone's practice, and I really hope this book serves that role for others as well, so that they don't feel so isolated in the work, so that they don't feel like they have to take it all on themselves or hold all the answers, because what we're doing is complicated and complex. We're not able, as individuals, to hold all the answers and hold that burden for social change. In critical work, we need each other, and we need that connection. So, I found this process to be really valuable in that sense.

Frankie

What I've gained from the process of working together has been incredible. We're in community with one another and everyone's expertise is really valued. There isn't a hierarchy. It's creating accessibility for people to participate in academic work, who normally wouldn't be able to. I think this is a way that we can bring more people into the academic world and break down this idea that only certain people can do it. We can feel so isolated as social workers and not having solidarity and support. We've got clinical supervision, and I know social workers come together, but the cooperative inquiry allowed for another way to do that and come together as a community. A lot of things might go as unnoticed acts of resistance. That's what makes community more important than ever right now, re-focusing on what's in our control, trying to see what we can do locally and trying to focus there.

Iris

Cooperative Inquiry is always helpful because like-minded social workers who have similar challenges are able to talk through them. When you hear how we have managed power or the ways that they have resisted the system to benefit clients, the way we navigate these really complex systems, the way that we advocate for our clients and bring their views to the forefront, it has helped me to see again how effective we are in this space. I've learned a lot about the different ways in which we engage in our work. It's so nice, because it centres the experiences and the reflections of people. It's not focused on the research or what the literature says. I mean, that's part of it, but it's focused on what people have to say. You can go about your day, continuing to work over years and years, and you don't stop and reflect and go wow! Look at all of this knowledge and skill that has been developed over that time.

Sarah

The discussions have opened up the idea that clinical social work is not the whole story, and it's not the only thing that's happening in mental health social work. It's been great to engage with these political conversations and to consider resistance and possibilities. There can be comfort in critique, when we position ourselves as though we're not part of the problem. We can try to separate ourselves from the mental health system, but actually we are all part of it. So, the question is, now what? In the ongoing process, there has been value in sitting with discomfort and making ourselves accountable, and it has been pertinent to recognise that there are diverse answers to the 'now what?' question. There's something really promising about it—that as a collective, we bring different skill-sets and attributes, and we make these diverse contributions, that together, are meaningful.

Beatrice

The quality of social work practice varies but many of us have been holding a line between transformation and complicity. Landing of both sides of this see-saw. Having a respectful forum to hear and grapple with struggles and successes in these endeavours honours our individual and collective practice wisdom. It also means we can ultimately theorise from the expertise of practice wisdom, recognising the diversity and messiness of practice that needs to be uniquely tailored to situations. It's been deeply inspiring to come together in fostering this space with colleagues.

Conclusion

Recognising a 'critical/clinical binary' as unhelpful (Bland et al., 2021), we sought to investigate and document mental health social work practice that is influenced by analyses of power. In doing so, we acknowledged the risks of complacency and being drawn into complicity with dominant knowledge systems, when social workers assume that the articulation of 'person-centred' and 'trauma-informed' practices in and of itself addresses injustices. While mental health social work is complex and contested, by unpacking the contradictions and paradoxes, this book makes visible the tensions in navigating mental health services and in finding spaces for resistance and creativity. Opportunities for critical mental health social work practice were explored, with a discussion of the politics of naming and responding to distress. A range of reflections and practice examples were shared to identify and examine how social workers navigate oppressive practices. The possibilities for mental health social work in working more collectively with groups and in solidarity with communities were also investigated, alongside working towards broader systems transformation. We argue that social work has a role to play in bringing an astute power analysis, to acknowledge and respond to the social structures that perpetuate distress. This role does not exist in a vacuum, but can be seen as part of a broader picture of myriad interconnected actions and justice-doing, extending far beyond mental health systems, in which people and communities are challenging status quo power relations and re-imagining the world and each other. Moving beyond resistance, we hope these diverse and collective reflections can open possibilities for change and radical hope. In fact, the beauty of this project has been the opportunity to critically reflect together, and in doing so, to embody the change we hope for.

References

Bland, R., Drake, G., Drayton, J., & Tullgren, A. (2021). Social work practice in mental health: An introduction (3rd ed.). Routledge. https://doi.org/10.4324/9781003148913

Egan, M., Friedman, V. J., Jones, D. R., Rhew, N. D., Robinson, S., & Sama, L. M. (2024). Restorative action research: Fostering wellbeing as a collective, relational, vital endeavor. *Action Research*. Online first: https://doi.org/10.1177/14767503241303834.

McKenzie-Mohr, S., & Lafrance, M. N. (2017). Narrative resistance in social work research and practice: Counter-storying in the pursuit of social justice. *Qualitative Social Work, 16*(2), 189–201.

Medina, J. (2013). *The epistemology of resistance: Gender and racial oppression, epistemic injustice, and the social imagination*. Oxford University Press.

Palmer, M., White, P., & Wooltorton, S. (2018). Embodying our future through collaboration: The change is in the doing. *The Journal of Environmental Education, 49*(4), 309–317.

Roper, C., Edan, V., Joffee-Kohn, N., Hamilton, B. & Gooding, P. (2023). *Abolitionist perspectives: Project report.* https://healthsciences.unimelb.edu.au/__data/assets/pdf_file/0007/5063497/CMHN_Abolition_Perspectives_Report.pdf

Index

L. Whitaker et al., *Social Work in the Mental Health Field*, SpringerBriefs in Social Work, https://doi.org/10.1007/978-3-032-08306-7

MIX
Papier aus verantwortungsvollen Quellen
Paper from responsible sources
FSC® C105338

If you have any concerns about our products,
you can contact us on
ProductSafety@springernature.com

In case Publisher is established outside the EU,
the EU authorized representative is:
Springer Nature Customer Service Center GmbH
Europaplatz 3, 69115 Heidelberg, Germany

Printed by Libri Plureos GmbH
in Hamburg, Germany